'Tales from the Tale'

A 'Whale' of a Guide to Seafood Cookery

Chef/Owner
Philip Andriano

Order this book online at www.trafford.com
or email orders@trafford.com

Most Trafford titles are also available at major online book retailers.

Printed in the United States of America.

ISBN: 978-1-4907-1946-7 (sc)
ISBN: 978-1-4907-1947-4 (e)

Library of Congress Control Number: 2013920693

Because of the dynamic nature of the Internet, any web addresses or links contained in this book may have changed since publication and may no longer be valid. The views expressed in this work are solely those of the author and do not necessarily reflect the views of the publisher, and the publisher hereby disclaims any responsibility for them.

Any people depicted in stock imagery provided by Thinkstock are models, and such images are being used for illustrative purposes only.
Certain stock imagery © Thinkstock.

Trafford rev. 11/07/2013

www.trafford.com
North America & international
toll-free: 1 888 232 4444 (USA & Canada)
fax: 812 355 4082

Dedication

If it weren't for dear old Mom and her Mother I suppose I never would have written this book
I would have never learned the values paired with the aesthetics of good cookery, thanks Mom and
Grandma
I also want to thank my family for eating whatever I cooked when developing the recipes and to my
dear friend Andy Stock for literally helping me put this book on paper.

Contents

Acknowledgement

By Proprietor/Owner
Sosh Andriano

'The Whales Tale'
"Hideaway on the Half Shell'"

You won't find us on Jericho Turnpike in a strip mall.
There is no billboard showing off our logo and we are not main stream USA
Chances are unless your friends told you where we are you won't find us.
The 'Whales Tale' was created by a laid back group of locals who love their community, great food and good friends!
Our menu was designed with one thing in mind. Fresh!!!!!
All of our fish is caught from local waters and brought up the dock each and every morning.
Our produce is harvested from our neighborhood farms and delivered to us every day.
We hope that each and every guest we meet will feel a sense of ownership in our dockside hideaway.
We want you to feel pride in sharing your secret local hangout spot with all of your friends.
Whether you're looking to have a bucket of corona's and watch the sun go down or take home a fresh flame grilled piece of fish we are always happy to see you!
We want you all to enjoy this book!
The manner in which it was written reflects my fathers' culinary expertise as an educator while developing the 'Tales' favorite recipes with you in mind.
And
While at the Whales Tale
Ask us about
HARBOR VIEW CATERING
81 FORT SALONGA ROAD
NORTHPORT, NY
From gala occasions to intimate wedding receptions,
Harbor View Catering at the Whale's Tale is renowned for exquisite food, spectacular presentation and first-class service.
Be it here, in the beautifully appointed waterfront catering room or in an off-site ballroom, or beach.
Harbor View Catering will make your every event unforgettable!

THE HARBOR VIEW
631-651-8844

Foreword

Phil Andriano got started cooking naturally. He's Italian. He grew up watching his grandmother and her sisters cook up a storm every weekend. His earliest memories include watching his grandmother preparing live snails in twelve quart pots and watching them try to crawl out and his grandmother smacking them back in with her big wooden spoon. Every Sunday was a marriage of flavors in the weekly feast.

At the age of fourteen, Phil started working in Italian delicatessens, preparing basic sauces, stocking shelves and slicing meats.

Following in his father's footsteps, he studied music first at Julliard and at Syracuse University and finally at the University of Hawaii. Ironically, his cooking is what paid his way through school. His real cooking experience started in Hawaii, cooking in various restaurants and hotels in Waikiki. He claims that his finest day was when he was accepted to the prestigious Culinary Institute of America in 1978. After making the trek east with his family, he graduated in 1981 and was on his way to being a professional chef.

Phil began his career as Sous Chef in charge of <u>Trumpets</u>, the nouveau cuisine restaurant at the Grand Hyatt in Manhattan. He later freelanced as chef de partier at places such as the <u>Four Seasons</u> Hotel in San Antonio and <u>Brennan's</u> in Houston. It was here that Phil developed much of his style in preparing seafood.

Phil returned to the New York area in 1984 and opened his own food service business. Phil worked for the New York Institute of Technology and New York Restaurant School as chef instructor. In 1985, he opened his three-star rated <u>Deep Sea Dive</u> in Port Washington. In 1988 Phil won the New York State Seafood Challenge and took the bronze medal at the American Seafood Challenge in Charleston, South Carolina later that year. <u>Deep Sea Dive</u> was named "Best Seafood Restaurant" on Long Island in 1989. In 1990, Phil was named one of the top five chefs on Long Island. Today, Phil was the chef/owner of the <u>Hook in Me Aye</u> cafe and clam bar in East Northport, New York where he gained accolades from the <u>New York Times</u> and <u>Long Island Newsday</u>. Other restaurants as chef owner were <u>In a Country Garden</u> in Glen Head, New York. Today he is partner, with his son Sosh, of the popular and well acclaimed <u>Whales Tale Café</u> in which these recipes were created for your enjoyment.

Introduction

Call me Ishmael . . . . wait this is not a novel about a whale, it's a cookbook about recipes developed at the 'Whales Tale Café'! Keep reading . . . .

I've always wanted to write a cookbook and share some of my favorite recipes, but I also feel that it is very important for a good cookbook to include some very basic aspects of cooking. In his foreword to <u>New Professional Chef</u>, Ferdinand E. Metz states that we "must learn lessons of greater value and wider application than a single recipe could provide." He talks of the need to be able to "grill, roast and poach" and I might add "sauté, deep fry, blacken and pan fry" to the list. So, what I've done here is create a chapter for each of these basic methods of cookery and illustrated each with some recipes and recipe variations. I have added a chapter on pan smoking which is a method I developed for fatty fishes such as tuna, salmon, mackerel and others. There are also chapters on pan stewing, stir frying, and oven poaching and cooking mediums. The chapters appear in order of what I believe should be learned first. In each chapter, methods of cookery by steps are illustrated.

I illustrate these methods with seafood recipes because that is where I've received most of my recognition. I want to discuss seafood also because it's expensive and I think it's a shame to have people go out and spend money on seafood, take it home and then destroy it because they lack certain basic cooking skills. My mother Ida is a great cook but can not deal with fish. As a child, every Friday, I had to endure intensely overcooked, dehydrated cod in some unspeakable tomato sauce. The delicate flavor of seafood must be maintained, not drowned out.

Each recipe is divided into steps of preparation which is the method I'm trying to convey and a list of ingredients required during each step. I write each recipe for two servings because if you are as bad at math as I am, it is easier to turn a recipe for two into a recipe for eight than it is to turn a recipe for eight into a recipe for two. Also when you try out a recipe, you probably want a small audience so I have downsized the recipes for use by the home kitchen cook. Each recipe also contains "notes" for each step. These should be referred to before attempting the recipe. These notes give some reason behind the directions or act as "technical standpoints" or safety warnings. These notes can provide the reader with enlightenment about the recipe and the method.

I also want to avoid being strict in recipes. The problem with most chefs' cookbooks is that they are too technical, too egocentric and too inflexible. Most recipes are tested in large restaurant kitchens, not in the home. Home cooks can have trouble with the size and complexity of a chef's recipe or simply do not have available some of the more esoteric ingredients. You know that guy who paints on TV with the beard and curly hair? I watch him. He's great. Once in a while he says "let's get a little crazy" and he takes paints from his palette and uses them in what seems to be a helter-skelter fashion, but when the painting is done, it looks great and I say to myself "hey! That's how I cook!" I like to get a little crazy, and when I do, it usually turns out OK. So, let's get a little crazy . . .

Sautéing

In the culinary schools in which I taught, we first tackled sautéing and stir frying because the first step one takes when one prepares most meals with vegetables, fish and meats is to sear or sauté the product.

The word sauté literally mean "jump" As the word implies, the sauté pan or "sauteuse" must be kept "jumping" in order to insure the product is cooked evenly. One way of doing that is to practice with a sauté pan off the fire by putting dried beans into the pan, tilt the pan forward, and then flick your wrist so that the beans jump to the rear of the pan. Keep practicing this maneuver until you get a smooth flow. Constant, smooth movement is important for uniform cooking. **Please don't sauté with hot fat until you can do your bean practice without spilling any beans.** If hot fat lands on you while you're sautéing, you will get a second degree burn. The handle of the sauteuse is also hot, but gloves are cumbersome. Use a light towel to handle the pan. Another way of achieving proficiency with a sauteuse is simply to watch a chef on TV and imitate him or her.

Sautéing is used when a product's juices are to be seared in to retain flavor and moisture. Sautéing also causes the natural flavors of the product to be released into the pan. Sautéing also results in a process known as caramelizing, which is simply the release of the natural sugars which then brown and add color (e.g. the golden brown of an onion or garlic) to the product. Proper sautéing requires that the product not be burnt in the process. Burning during the t step causes bitterness and gives an off-color to the product.

Because it is done so quickly, the sauté method is meant for small pieces of seafood . . . Shrimp, scallops or shucked mollusks are small and firm enough to be sautéed whole. Larger fish needs to be sliced or escalloped into sauté sized pieces. The sauté method should be used only on fish with firm flesh such as swordfish, monkfish, grouper, tuna or shark. Sauté is not a good method for fish that are too delicate or flaky such as flounder, cod or salmon.

An important concept to consider when sautéing is what is known in French as "mise en place" which means "putting in place." This concept indicates the extreme importance of having everything needed for cooking prepared and readily available before beginning the actual cooking process. To start to sauté a meal and stop to peel or cut up a carrot is not feasible. The Larousse Gastronome states: "When all these small tasks are done, and all the operations preceding the actual cooking completed, the work of cooking is much simplified." The recipes included in this book are laid out in steps so that the effecting of "mise en place" can be accomplished. The "INGREDIENTS" section of each recipe tells what ingredients should be at hand for each step of the recipe.

Sautéing must take place in a **small amount** of fat. "Fat" can mean such things as animal fat, butter, margarine, vegetable oils, olive oil or seed oils. Which "fat" one uses should be dictated by the product being sautéed and/or the ethnic origin of the recipe and/or health considerations. For instance, shrimp prepared Cajun style should be sautéed in fatback, which is literally fat off a pig's back. Shrimp prepared in an Italian method such as scampi would be sautéed in olive oil. Yet oriental shrimp would be stir fired in sesame oil and soy oil, same shrimp, but totally different flavors. I hasten to add that substituting a vegetable fat for an animal fat for health or personal reasons (monounsaturated fats, like olive oil is healthiest) or for "whatever blows your hair back" is perfectly all right provided you can accept a non traditional taste.

The method of sautéing, as do all cooking methods, consists of several steps which will be illustrated by the following recipes. Sautéing is sometimes only the first step in preparing a course. Other times, an entire entree is prepared within the sautés and usually finished in a sauce. Such an entree is;

Sea Scallops with Cracked Peppercorns and Anisette

<u>Yield</u>: 2 servings

INGREDIENTS

Step one:	Fat (olive oil)	2tsp
	Minced garlic	½ tsp
	Chopped onion	1Tb
Step two:	Sea scallops	12oz
	Cracked black peppercorns	½ tsp
	Granulated sugar	½ tsp
	Anisette	1oz (a shot)
Step three:	Prepared tomato sauce	1Tb
	Prepared beef stock (bouillon)	2oz
	Half and half cream	1oz
	Salt	to taste
	Thyme	a pinch

Nutrition Facts
Amount per Serving
Calories 307.1
Total Fat 8.3 g
Saturated Fat 1.7 g
Polyunsaturated Fat 0.5 g
Monounsaturated Fat 3.8 g
Cholesterol 75.6 mg
Sodium 422.6 mg
Potassium 112.0 mg
Total Carbohydrate 8.4 g
Dietary Fiber 0.2 g
Sugars 6.5 g
Protein 35.3 g

METHOD

<u>Step one</u>: In a sauté pan, place the fat over high heat. As soon as the fat has heated, add the garlic and then the onion in that order, sauté until translucent.

<u>Step two</u>: Add the sea scallops, peppercorns and sugar. Sauté until the scallops are golden and seared. Remove the sauté pan from fire and pour in the shot of anisette. The anisette should vaporize (steam). Return the pan to the fire. At this point you may or may not have a flash of fire if the alcohol ignites. Whether it fires or not, does not affect the recipe, just don't blow yourself up. At this point, remove the scallops from the pan and set them aside.

<u>Step three</u>: Add the tomato sauce, the beef stock, half and half cream, salt and thyme to the pan and return to the fire. Reduce sauce by 1/2. Then return the scallops to the pan and further reduce until the sauce coats the scallops. Put 'em on some herbal or plain rice. Then, eat 'em.

NOTES

<u>Step one</u>:

A-The smoking point of oil is higher than butter. Any fat should not be heated past the smoking point because above the smoking point, the oil will not brown the garlic and onions, it will burn them.

B-Put the garlic in before the onions because what you are looking for is a golden color from the garlic. You can actually smell the release of the garlic's essence. Then add onions, whose released water content will further prevent the garlic from burning.

Step two:

A-When the scallops are removed from the pan and set aside; they should not be fully cooked, just seared. They will tend to "weep" juices, so put them in a bowl rather than on a flat dish. Don't throw out or drain off the juice.

B-We are just kidding about blowing yourself up, but do be careful not to put your face over the pan when returning it to the fire.

C-I am **not** kidding about the importance **of taking the pan off the fire before you add the alcohol**. If you add the alcohol to a pan on the fire, you really can blow up!

Step three:

A-The prepared sauce, stocks and liquids used in this and other recipes are known as "cooking mediums" from which sauces are made. In this recipe it's the sauce for the scallops. They can be store bought, but if you want, can be homemade. Stocks can be made and frozen in ice cube trays for incremental use.

Note: From step one to step three should take less than seven minutes.

Another entree which is made entirely in the sauteuse is:

Scampi with Garlic, Basil, Black Olives and Fresh Tomato

<u>Yield:</u> 2 servings

INGREDIENTS

Step one:	Fat (olive oil)	2tsp
	Minced garlic	½ tsp
	Chopped onion	1Tb
	Granulated sugar	½ tsp
Step two:	Medium shrimp peeled and cleaned	12 ea (12oz)
	Flour	1Tb
	Sliced black olives	2Tb
	Diced fresh tomato	¼ cp
	Minced fresh basil	1Tb
Step three:	Prepared fish stock (bouillon)	2oz
	White wine	2oz (2 shots)
	Half and half cream	2oz

Nutrition Facts

Amount per Serving
Calories 362.5
Total Fat 14.1 g
Saturated Fat 4.5 g
Polyunsaturated Fat 1.7 g
Monounsaturated Fat 5.3 g
Cholesterol 275.1 mg
Sodium 444.6 mg
Potassium 489.4 mg
Total Carbohydrate 15.2 g
Dietary Fiber 0.4 g
Sugars 3.2 g
Protein 37.5 g

METHOD

<u>Step one:</u> In a sauté pan, place the oil over high heat. As soon as the oil becomes heated, add the garlic, the onions and the sugar in that order, cook until translucent and golden brown.

<u>Step two:</u> Immediately, add the shrimp. Sauté until seared. Remove shrimp from pan and reserve. Add pinch of flour to pan along with olives, tomato and basil.

<u>Step three:</u> Add the stock, wine, heavy cream, salt and pepper to the pan and return the pan to the fire. Reduce sauce by 1/2. Then, return the shrimp to the pan and further reduce until the sauce coats the shrimp. Put 'em on some risotto or orzo pasta or linguine. Then, eat 'em.

NOTES

<u>Step one:</u>

A-As stated, the smoking point of olive oil is slightly higher than butter. Knowing the heating capacity that various fats can endure is an important part of successful sautéing. As you work with different recipes, you will become more familiar with these temperatures.

B-As in the last recipe, put the garlic before the onions because you are looking for a golden color of the garlic and you can actually smell the release of the essence of the garlic. Then add the onions, whose released water content will further prevent the garlic from burning.

C-The pinch of sugar will enhance the caramelizing process of the sauté method and will neutralize the acids in the wine which is added in step three.

<u>Step two:</u>

A-When the shrimp are removed from the pan and set aside; they will not weep as did the scallops. They must be firm but tender to the touch and completely cooked. Thirty seconds is usually all that is required in a hot olive oil medium. Don't overcook the shrimp as they will shrink and dry up.

B-The flour added to the hot oil acts as a thickening agent and when the liquids are added, a sauce begins to form.

<u>Step three:</u>

A-As before, these prepared stocks and liquids are what are known as "cooking mediums" from which the sauce for the shrimp are made and complete the cooking process. They can be store bought or home made. Stocks can be made and frozen in ice cube trays for incremental use.

B-The optional use of heavy cream will act as a glaze for the shrimp.

Note: From step one through step three should take less than five minutes.

Monkfish with Smoked Bacon Ragout

<u>Yield:</u> 2 servings

INGREDIENTS

Step one:	Fat (packaged bacon)	¼ cp (raw)
	Minced garlic	1tsp
	Coarsely chopped onion	¼ cp
	Granulated sugar	½ tsp
Step two:	Thinly (1/4") sliced monkfish	8pc/1oz ea
	Flour	2Tb
	Sweet peppers (red, yellow, green)	¼ cp
	Diced fresh tomato	¼ cp
	Minced fresh basil	1Tb
	Thyme leaves	a pinch
Step three:	Prepared beef stock (bouillon)	½ cp/4oz
	Prepared tomato sauce	¼ cp
	Red wine	2oz (2 shots)
	Salt and red pepper flakes	(to taste)

Nutrition Facts

Amount per Serving
Calories 309.2
Total Fat 5.0 g
Saturated Fat 0.7 g
Polyunsaturated Fat 0.5 g
Monounsaturated Fat 3.4 g
Cholesterol 0.0 mg
Sodium 251.4 mg
Potassium 339.5 mg
Total Carbohydrate 23.4 g
Dietary Fiber 2.4 g
Sugars 4.2 g
Protein 3.3 g

METHOD

<u>Step one:</u> In a large sauté pan, place the bacon over high heat. Render the fat out without burning the bacon. Remove and reserve the cooked bacon. Leave in fry pan. Add garlic, onions and sugar as in previous recipes.

<u>Step two:</u> Immediately, add the slices of monkfish. Sauté until seared. Remove monkfish from pan and reserve. Add flour to the pan. Let the flour cook out <u>over a lower heat</u> until golden brown. Now, add peppers, tomato, basil and thyme. Cook for an additional thirty seconds.

<u>Step three:</u> Add the stock, prepared tomato sauce, wine, salt and pepper flakes to the pan. Then return the monkfish to the pan and reduce until the sauce coats the monkfish. Add the bacon. Put it on "dirty rice" (see note) and serve with corn bread. Then eat it.

NOTES

<u>Step one:</u>

A-Rendered oil from the bacon serves as our cooking medium. Any saturated fat like bacon <u>will smoke at a much lower temperature</u> than the olive oil of previous recipes, so be careful not to scorch it or it will turn the dish bitter.

Step two:

A-As in the sauté recipes, the flour added to the hot oil acts as a thickening agent. But in this recipe, it is important to cook out the flour over <u>low heat</u>, creating a hazel brown roux. In classic Cajun cooking, the thickening agent (roux) is always further cooked.

Step three:

A-The heat of the pan needs to be <u>lower here</u> than in sauté recipes and <u>dropped to a simmer</u>.

B-The "dirty rice" is a classic Cajun accompaniment consisting of vegetables, chicken liver, and sautéed together then added to white rice. You know how to sauté now, so make your own "dirty rice" recipe to suit your taste.

Note: From step one to step three should take little more than ten minutes.

Note: The larger pieces of seafood and the increased amount of liquid in this recipe make it almost a pan stewing recipe rather than a sauté recipe.

Pan Stewing

Pan stewing is similar to sautéing except that the time of reduction is increased because the presence of more liquid and larger pieces of product. The amount of liquid is such that it is no longer a sauce but really a stew, where the product is enveloped in a larger amount of liquid. The consistency of the liquid is the result of what kind of effect you are trying to create. A bouillabaisse is considered a lighter stew consisting of a bouillon and an infusion of herbs along with the seafood while a ragout is a thicker stew which can consist of a purée of tomatoes and/or other garden vegetables.

The first step in pan stewing is the sauté process. Once the sautéing is done, and the seafood, vegetables and cooking medium are added to the pan the cooking time is increased. Unlike sautéing, pan stewing finishes the product over a lower heat. It is simmered so the flavors of the products have time to be released and marry in the medium. The liquid is now considered not a sauce but rather part of a finished stew.

We use the word "stew" here to mean a meal cooked within a large amount of liquid. Many people think of a stew as something that is cooked in a large pot over several hours of low heat which of course is correct. Pan stewing creates much the same kind of meal as a potted stew, but takes far less time. Consider these recipes the first of which is a bouillabaisse style which has a slightly thickened sauce using a roux of oil and flour, the second of which is a thicker ragout style recipe getting its thickening through a vegetable purée and in the third of which a pasta is cooked directly in a sauce instead of being boiled first and the sauce added later:

Northport Shellfish Stew

Yield: 2 servings
INGREDIENTS

Step one:	Fat (olive oil)	2tsp
	Minced garlic	1tsp
	Coarsely chopped onion	¼ cp
	Granulated sugar	a pinch
	Flour	2Tbs.
Step two:	Mussels in shell, well cleaned	2dz
	Littleneck clams in shell-well cleaned	1dz
	Sea scallops	½ dz
	Shrimp peeled and cleaned	½ dz
	Firm fleshed fish (ex. monk, cat, tuna)	4oz
	Sweet peppers (red, yellow, green)	¼ cp
	Minced fresh basil	1Tb
	Thyme leaves	a pinch
	Tarragon	a pinch
Step three:	Prepared chicken or fish stock (bouillon)	½ cp/4oz
	White wine	2oz (2 shots)
	Salt and pepper	(to taste)

Nutrition Facts

Amount per Serving
Calories 659.6
Total Fat 14.3 g
Saturated Fat 2.2 g
Polyunsaturated Fat 2.8 g
Monounsaturated Fat 5.1 g
Cholesterol 154.2 mg
Sodium 1,320.7 mg
Potassium 1,005.1 mg
Total Carbohydrate 40.9 g
Dietary Fiber 2.4 g
Sugars 7.2 g
Protein 70.3 g

METHOD

Step one: In a large sauté pan (12" or more) heat the oil and sauté the garlic, then onions. Reduce heat. Place the sugar and flour into the pan.

Step two: Place the mussels, clams, scallops, shrimp and fish into the pan. Continue with the peppers and herbs. Toss the product just long enough to coat everything with the oil and herbs.

Step three: Add the stock, wine and salt and pepper. Simmer over a low heat for 10 minutes or until all the clams and mussels open. Serve with garlic toast or good old French bread for dipping. Then eat it.

NOTES

Before preparation:

A-Check to make sure all the mussels and clams are alive. First, dispose of any mollusk which has a broken or cracked shell. If shells are closed, try to separate the shell by hand, just to check for "mudders" which are closed shells full of mud. If one of them gets into the stew, everything is ruined. If the shells are slightly open, they should close when tapped. If a mollusk with an open shell does not close to the touch, feed it to the cat. Finally, as with any seafood, the best way to check for freshness is to smell the product.

Step one:

   A-The sauté must be very quick. We do not want to caramelize (brown) the onions and garlic. We are looking for a light clear broth, not a brown broth.

Step two:

   A-The tossing of the product is only to coat it with the oil and herbs. The real cooking of the product takes place in step three (simmering of the stock). Step two, like step one is more a preparation than an actual cooking process.

   B-In a course which is sautéed the seafood is removed from the pan, set aside and returned once a sauce has been created by reduction. In pan stewing, the seafood remains in the pan to stew or simmer over a low heat and there is no significant reduction of liquid.

Step three:

   A-The difference between sautéing and pan stewing is here. We are simmering the product in liquid over low heat. The liquid is not reduced to a sauce but rather, remains a broth which is an integral part of the meal. Overcooking and burning, which is a potential problem in sautéing, is less likely here because we are simmering over low heat. Still, overcooking can occur, shrimp can dry up, fish can decompose, liquids can evaporate. Seven to ten minutes of simmering should do the job. Use the clams and mussels as a guide. When they open, the stew is done.

Note: From step one to step three should take less than twelve minutes.

Seafood Fra Diablo

<u>Yield:</u> 2 servings

INGREDIENTS

Step one:	Fat (olive oil)	2tsp
	Minced garlic	1tsp
	Coarsely chopped onion	¼ cp
	Granulated sugar	a pinch
Step two:	Mussels in shell, well cleaned	2dz
	Littleneck clams in shell, well cleaned	1dz
	Sea scallops	½ dz
	Shrimp peeled and cleaned	½ dz
	Firm fleshed fish (ex. <u>monk</u>, cat, tuna)	4oz
	Sweet peppers (red, yellow, green)	¼ cp
	Minced fresh basil	1Tb
	Oregano	a pinch
Step three:	Prepared chicken or fish stock	½ cp/4oz
	Prepared tomato sauce	½ cp
	Diced fresh tomato	¼ cp
	Red wine	2oz (2 shots)
	Salt	(to taste)
	Tabasco sauce	1Tb

Nutrition Facts

Amount per Serving
Calories 660.4
Total Fat 14.4 g
Saturated Fat 2.2 g
Polyunsaturated Fat 2.8 g
Monounsaturated Fat 5.1 g
Cholesterol 154.2 mg
Sodium 1,365.3 mg
Potassium 1,014.1 mg
Total Carbohydrate 41.0 g
Dietary Fiber 2.4 g
Sugars 7.2 g
Protein 70.4 g

METHOD

<u>Step one:</u> In a large sauté pan (12" or more) heat the olive oil over high heat and sauté the garlic and onions. Reduce heat. Place the sugar into the pan.

<u>Step two:</u> Place the mussels, clams, scallops, shrimp and fish into the pan. Continue with the peppers and herbs. Toss the product just long enough to coat everything with the olive oil and herbs.

<u>Step three:</u> Add the stock, tomato sauce, wine and salt and pepper. Simmer over a low heat for 10 minutes or until all the clams and mussels open. Serve over linguini and/or with garlic toast or good old French bread for dipping. Then eat it.

NOTES

<u>Before preparation:</u>

A-Check to make sure all the mussels and clams are alive. First, dispose of any mollusk which has a broken or cracked shell. If shells are closed, try to separate the shell by hand, just to check for "mudders" which are closed shells full of mud. If one of them gets into the stew, everything is ruined.

If the shells are slightly open, they should close when tapped. If a mollusk with an open shell does not close to the touch, feed it to the cat. Finally, as with any seafood, the best way to check for freshness is to smell the product.

Step one:

A-In this recipe, we are looking to caramelize the onions and garlic so the sauté process will be somewhat longer than in the previous recipe.

Step two:

A-The tossing of the product is only to coat it with the olive oil and herbs. The real cooking of the product takes place in step three (simmering of the stock). Step two is more a preparation than an actual cooking process.

B-In a course which is sautéed the seafood is removed from the pan, set aside and returned once a sauce has been created by reduction. In pan stewing, the seafood remains in the pan to stew or simmer over a low heat and there is no significant reduction of liquid.

Step three:

A-The difference between sautéing and pan stewing is here. We are simmering the product in liquid over low heat. The liquid is not reduced to a sauce but rather, remains a broth which is an integral part of the meal. Overcooking and burning, which is a potential problem in sautéing, is less likely here because we are simmering over low heat. Still, overcooking can occur, shrimp can dry up, fish can decompose, liquids can evaporate. Seven to ten minutes of simmering should do the job. Use the clams and mussels as a guide. When they open, the stew is done.

B-The olive oil and tomato sauce act as a thickening agent making this recipe more of a ragout than a bouillabaisse.

Note: From step one to step three should take less than fourteen minutes.

Sautéed Shrimp with Tortellini in a Pepperoni Cream

<u>Yield:</u> 2 servings

INGREDIENTS

Step one:		
	Fat (olive oil)	2tsp
	Minced garlic	1tsp
	Coarsely chopped onion	¼ cp
	Granulated sugar	a pinch
	Thin sliced pepperoni	1oz

Step two:		
	Shrimp peeled and cleaned (16/20)	1dz (16oz)
	Minced fresh basil	1Tb

Step three:		
	Prepared chicken stock (bouillon)	1cp/8oz
	Prepared tomato sauce	¼ cp
	White wine 2oz	(2 shots)
	Salt and red pepper flakes	(to taste)
	Frozen cheese tortellini	1cp
	Heavy cream	1oz

Nutrition Facts

Amount per Serving
Calories 589.3
Total Fat 21.9 g
Saturated Fat 7.6 g
Polyunsaturated Fat 2.4 g
Monounsaturated Fat 7.1 g
Cholesterol 394.7 mg
Sodium 940.4 mg
Potassium 650.8 mg
Total Carbohydrate 33.6 g
Dietary Fiber 2.7 g
Sugars 5.6 g
Protein 57.2 g

METHOD

<u>Step one:</u> In a large sauté pan (12" or more) heat the olive oil over high heat and sauté the garlic and onions. Reduce heat. Place the sugar and the pepperoni into the pan.

<u>Step two:</u> Place the shrimp into the pan. Continue with the basil. Toss the product just long enough to coat everything with the oil and basil.

<u>Step three:</u> Add the stock, tomato sauce, wine and salt and pepper, tortellini and cream. Remove and reserve the shrimp. Simmer for ten minutes or until tortellini is tender. Return the shrimp, and heat for another minute and serve.

NOTES

<u>Step one:</u>

A-In this recipe, we are looking to caramelize the onions and garlic in the sauté process.

<u>Step two:</u>

A-The tossing of the product is only to coat it with the oil and basil. The real cooking of the product takes place in step three (simmering of the stock). Step two is more a preparation than an actual cooking process.

B-In a course which is sautéed the seafood is removed from the pan, set aside and returned once a sauce has been created by reduction. In pan stewing, the seafood remains in the pan to stew or simmer over a low heat. In this recipe the shrimp should be removed because it is tender and fragile and should not be overcooked.

Step three:

A-The difference between sautéing and pan stewing is here. We are simmering the product in liquid over low heat. The liquid is not reduced to a sauce but rather, remains a broth which is an integral part of the meal. Overcooking and burning, which is a potential problem in sautéing, is less likely here because we are simmering over low heat. Still, overcooking can occur, shrimp can dry up, liquids can evaporate. Use the tortellini as a guide for cooking time. When the tortellini is tender, you are done.

B-The cream and tomato sauce act as thickening agent.

C-The tortellini is a frozen, raw product which does not need to be pre boiled. It can literally be added directly to the sauce in its raw state. Stewing the tortellini directly in the sauce instead of boiling it in water allows the tortellini to absorb the flavors from the sauce.

D-Unlike the last recipes, we want the liquid to be reduced further so that the liquid becomes a sauce and covers and coats the tortellini. Return the shrimp only long enough to insure it is reheated but not further cooked.

Note: From step one to step three should take less than fifteen minutes.

Steamers (Belly Clams) in a Broth of Caraway and Onions

Yield: 2 servings

INGREDIENTS

Step one:	Fat (olive oil/butter)	2tsp/1Tb
	Minced garlic	1tsp
	Coarsely chopped onion	¼ cp
Step two:	Soft shell clams, well cleaned	2dz/large size
	Caraway seed	1tsp
Step three:	Prepared chicken stock (bouillon)	1cp/8oz
	White wine or Beer	2oz (2 shots)
	Salt and red pepper flakes	to taste

Nutrition Facts

Amount per Serving
Calories 191.1
Total Fat 6.2 g
Saturated Fat 0.8 g
Polyunsaturated Fat 0.8 g
Monounsaturated Fat 3.6 g
Cholesterol 48.0 mg
Sodium 803.7 mg
Potassium 693.7 mg
Total Carbohydrate 7.0 g
Dietary Fiber 0.5 g
Sugars 0.7 g
Protein 21.7 g

METHOD

Step one: In a large sauté pan (12" or more) heat the olive oil and butter over high heat and sauté the garlic and onions. Reduce heat.

Step two: Place the steamers into the pan. Continue with the caraway seed. Toss the product just long enough to coat everything with the oil and butter.

Step three: Add the stock, wine or beer, then salt and pepper. Simmer for ten minutes or until the clams open slightly and are tender.

NOTES

Step one:
A-In this recipe, we are looking to caramelize the onions and garlic in the sauté process.

Step two:
A-The tossing of the product is only to coat it with the oil and caraway. The real cooking of the product takes place in step three (simmering of the stock). Step two is more a preparation than an actual cooking process.
B-In a course which is sautéed, the seafood is removed from the pan, set aside and returned once a sauce has been created by reduction. In pan stewing, the seafood remains in the pan to stew or simmer over a low heat.

Step three:
A-The difference between sautéing and pan stewing is here. We are simmering the product in liquid over low heat. The liquid is not reduced to a sauce but rather, remains a broth which is an integral part of the meal. Overcooking and burning, which is a potential problem in sautéing, is less likely here because we are simmering over low heat. Still, overcooking can occur, clams can dry up, liquids can evaporate.

Note: From step one to step three should take less than ten minutes.

New England Crab and Corn Sunset Chowder

Yield; 2 servings

INGREDIENTS

Step one:		
	Fat (olive oil/butter)	2tsp/1Tb
	Flour (AP)	1Tb
	Garlic (minced)	1tsp
	Onion (diced)	¼ cp

Step two:		
	Pulled blue claw crab meat	2oz
	Surimi (imitation crab meat)	2oz
	Potatoes (diced)	¼ cp
	Carrots (diced)	¼ cp
	Celery (diced)	¼ cp
	Thyme	1tsp
	Corn kernels (frozen)	¼ cp

Step three:		
	Clam juice	2cp
	Half and Half	½ cp

Nutrition Facts

Amount per Serving
Calories 374.7
Total Fat 12.3 g
Saturated Fat 5.1 g
Polyunsaturated Fat 0.8 g
Monounsaturated Fat 5.4 g
Cholesterol 61.1 mg
Sodium 1,260.9 mg
Potassium 623.5 mg
Total Carbohydrate 50.6 g
Dietary Fiber 2.3 g
Sugars 1.9 g
Protein 11.9 g

METHOD

Step one: In a Sauce pan (8" or more) heat the olive oil and butter over high heat and sauté the garlic and onions. Reduce heat. Stir in the flour to make a roux (thickening agent).

Step two: Place the crab and Surimi into the pan. Continue with the potatoes, carrots, celery, thyme and corn. Toss the product just long enough to coat everything with the oil and butter.

Step three: Add the clam juice and the half and half, then salt and pepper. Simmer for ten minutes or until you have made soup.

NOTES

Step one:

A-In this recipe, we are looking to caramelize the onions and garlic in the sauté process.

Step two:

A-The tossing of the product is only to coat it with the oil. The real cooking of the product takes place in step three (simmering of the soup). Step two is more a preparation than an actual cooking process, but necessary to cook out the roux.

B-In a course which is sautéed, the seafood is removed from the pan, set aside and returned once a sauce has been created by reduction. In pan stewing, the seafood remains in the pan to stew or simmer over a low heat, the end product soup. Chowder is any soup that has potatoes in it.

<u>Step three</u>:

A-The difference between sautéing and pan stewing is here. We are simmering the product in liquid over low heat. The liquid is not reduced to a sauce but rather, remains a thickened broth which is an integral part of the meal. Overcooking and burning, which is a potential problem in sautéing, is less likely here because we are simmering over low heat.

Note: From step one to step three should take less than ten minutes, or until vegetables are tender.

Stir Frying

Stir frying is the Asian equivalent of Sautéing, which is a European method. The pan used in true stir frying is the "Wok" which is comparable to the sauteuse used in the sauté method. The wok has high sides and no extended handles so the pan cannot be operated like a sauteuse. The movement of the food in the wok is effected, not by tossing the pan, but by use of large spoon or ladle like oriental utensil known as a Chan. It is important although not critical to use a wok in stir frying. The wok is made out of steel and so is better than an aluminum sauteuse because the steel maintains high heat much better than aluminum. The wok concentrates its heat in the center of the pan while the sauteuse distributes the heat more evenly. But if you only have a pan, use it. It is interesting to note that the basic principles of sauté and stir fry are the same (i.e. the use of a very hot fat, the small pieces of the ingredients and the creation of a sauce directly in the pan all apply.) The real difference between stir fry and sauté lies in the ingredients. Stir fry recipes usually contain products which are indigenous to the Orient such as ginger root, bamboo shoots, water chestnuts, cashews etc. in addition to traditional western vegetables like garlic, onions and tomatoes. The gathering of these ingredients or as we called it before, the "mise en place" is important in each step. Stir frying takes place so quickly that it is very important that everything that is to be cooked is available before a wok is heated. Here I want to extend the concept of "mise en place" into the cooking process itself. The order in which each ingredient goes into the pan is important. Perhaps a phrase like "mise en temps" would be appropriate.

Stir frying usually takes place in oils that have high smoking points and so can withstand very high temperatures such as peanut oil, soy oil, and sesame oil. Sesame oil is rarely used alone. It has a strong but very pleasant taste, evaporates quickly and is very expensive so it is usually blended with other vegetable oils.

As in sautéing, the size of the product is important. The size of each morsel of food should be about the same to insure even cooking. Knowing the cooking times of each different type of food is important too. A piece of carrot will take a lot longer to cook that a much larger piece of broccoli, so carrots should be in the pan before the broccoli. As a rule, the green vegetables go in last so they retain their color and texture.

Marinating is an important part of stir frying as well. This is because the cooking is done so quickly and the more flavor you can get into the main product the better. Marinating is an excellent way of adding or enhancing flavor. In the recipes below the marinating process is described in a "preparation step."

The completion of the stir fry method is the sauce. As in sautéing, the sauce is made right in the pan. In sautéing the thickening agent is a roux. In stir frying it is known as "slurry" of corn starch and a liquid which could be chicken stock, fish stock, sherry wine or sometimes just water. The slurry is created at the last moment and thickens to make a light sauce. In addition to the sauce, flavor enhancers such as prepared oyster sauce, soy sauce, sesame oil and teriyaki etc. can be used to create your own effect. You can go on to create your own recipes once you understand the basic cooking methods. But to get you started, here are three stir fry recipes.

Sesame Shrimp with Water Chestnuts and Scallions

Yield: 2 servings
INGREDIENTS

Preparation Step:	Shrimp cleaned and peeled (16/20)	1dz (12oz)
(Marinade)	Dry sherry	2oz (2 shots)

Step one:	Fat (soy oil)	2tsp
	Fat (sesame oil)	1tsp
	Minced garlic	1tsp
	Coarsely chopped onion	¼ cp
	Granulated sugar	½ tsp
	Grated ginger root	½ tsp

Step two:	Marinated shrimp	1dz
	Water chestnuts	1small can
	Red bell peppers (diced)	¼ cp

Step three:	Reserved marinade (sherry)	2oz
	Prepared chicken stock (bouillon)	½ cp (4oz)
	Salt and red pepper flakes	(to taste)
	Prepared soy sauce	2Tb
	Prepared oyster sauce	1Tb
	Minced scallions	3Tb
	Toasted sesame seed	1tsp

Step four:	Corn starch slurry (see notes)	¼ cp = 1Tb to 2oz

Nutrition Facts

Amount per Serving
Calories 377.5
Total Fat 10.9 g
Saturated Fat 1.7 g
Polyunsaturated Fat 3.0 g
Monounsaturated Fat 5.0 g
Cholesterol 258.4 mg
Sodium 1,749.1 mg
Potassium 766.6 mg
Total Carbohydrate 26.5 g
Dietary Fiber 2.7 g
Sugars 4.0 g
Protein 37.7 g

METHOD

Preparation step: Put the shrimp into the sherry and let marinate while you are arranging and preparing other ingredients.

Step one: Combine the soy and sesame oils. In a preheated standard 14" wok, place the combined oils and over high heat, stir fry the garlic and onions and ginger root for thirty seconds. Reduce heat. Place the sugar into the pan.

Step two: Drain the shrimp. Strain and reserve the marinade. Place the shrimp into the pan and caramelize. Add water chestnuts and red bell peppers. Stir fry for three minutes or until shrimp are firm.

Step three: Add the stock, reserved marinade, salt and pepper, soy and oyster sauces, scallions and sesame seeds.

<u>Step four</u>: Using the Chan, move the food up the side of the wok and immediately add corn starch slurry to the liquids in the center of the wok and continue stirring. When slurry thickens to a sauce and is clear, remove everything and serve over steamed rice.

NOTES
<u>General</u>:
   A-Unless a cooking time is noted, go immediately from one step to the next.

<u>Preparation step</u>:
   A-Marinating is a method used to tenderize and season the product before cooking.
   B-Dry "cooking" sherry is not as acceptable as dry sherry for a marinade because of the high salt content and inferior quality. However it is less expensive and doesn't require a trip to the liquor store. Don't use a sweet or cream sherry.

<u>Step one</u>:
   A-We are looking to caramelize the garlic onions ginger root and sugar in that order.

<u>Step two</u>:
   A-The stirring of the product is only to coat it with the oils and the existing flavors.

<u>Step three</u>:
   A-No real cooking time is needed for the liquids in step three. There is no need for reduction of liquid here. The sauce is provided by the slurry in step four.
   B-No real cooking time is needed for the sesame seeds or scallions which are added for color enhancement and are considered a garnish.

<u>Step four</u>:
   A-The corn starch slurry is made of one part corn starch to four parts liquid. The liquid chosen can be chicken stock, water, sherry, or what ever suits your taste. If unsure, use water.
   B-The slurry thickens the product within a very short period of time and is finished only when the sauce is clear.

Note: Cooking time should not exceed five minutes.

Yellow Fin Tuna Teriyaki

Yield: 2 servings

INGREDIENTS

Preparation Step:	Cubed yellow fin tuna	1lb
	Teriyaki sauce	2oz
	Rice wine	1oz
Step one:	Marinated tuna	1lb
	Fat (peanut oil)	2tsp
	Fat (sesame seed oil)	1tsp
Step two:	Minced garlic	1tsp
	Coarsely chopped onion	¼ cp
	Granulated sugar	a pinch
	Grated ginger root	½ tsp
Step three:	Reserved marinade	2oz
	Prepared chicken stock (bouillon)	¼ cp
	Salt and red pepper flakes	to taste
	Prepared soy sauce	2Tb
	Prepared oyster sauce	1Tb
	Minced scallions	3Tb
Step four:	Corn starch slurry (see notes)	¼ cp = 1Tb to 2oz water

Nutrition Facts

Amount per Serving
Calories 325.8
Total Fat 8.4 g
Saturated Fat 1.3 g
Polyunsaturated Fat 1.8 g
Monounsaturated Fat 4.5 g
Cholesterol 65.7 mg
Sodium 2,764.8 mg
Potassium 823.2 mg
Total Carbohydrate 18.0 g
Dietary Fiber 0.5 g
Sugars 6.2 g
Protein 37.6 g

METHOD

Preparation step: Put the cubed tuna into the teriyaki and rice wine, let marinate while you are arranging and preparing other ingredients.

Step one: Remove tuna from marinade. Strain and reserve the marinade. Combine the peanut and sesame oils. In a preheated standard 14" wok, place the combined oils and over high heat, stir fry the tuna just long enough to sear it. Then remove the tuna and set aside.

Step two: To the oil in the wok add the garlic, onion, granulated sugar and grated ginger root. Stir fry for thirty seconds.

Step three: Add the stock, reserved marinade, salt and pepper, soy and oyster sauces and scallions.

Step four: Using the Chan, stir the contents of the wok and immediately add corn starch slurry and continue stirring. When slurry thickens to a sauce and is clear, return the tuna to the pan just long enough to reheat it. Remove everything and serve over steamed rice or cellophane noodles.

NOTES
General:
 A-Unless a cooking time is noted, go immediately from one step to the next.

Preparation step:
 A-Marinating is a method used to tenderize and season the product before cooking.

Step one:
 A-Our object here is only to sear the natural juices into the tuna. If we caramelize (brown) the garlic and onions first, and then add the tuna, the juices from the garlic and onions will steam the tuna and we don't want that because it would tend to make the tuna tough.

Step two:
 A-Caramelize the garlic first, then the onions, then the ginger root and finally, add the sugar. This will turn into a nice little glaze. Adding a little vinegar (2 tsp.) will give you a sweet-sour effect.

Step three:
 A-No real cooking time is needed for the liquids in step three. There is no need for reduction of liquid here. The sauce is provided by the slurry in step four.

Step four:
 A-The corn starch slurry is made of one part corn starch to four parts liquid. The liquid chosen can be chicken stock, water, sherry, or what ever suits your taste. If unsure, use water.
 B-The slurry thickens the product within a very short period of time and is finished only when the sauce is clear. The tuna is added after the sauce clears and is heated only briefly. Because of the delicate flavor of the fish, tuna should be eaten rare to pink in the middle. For those who insist on medium to well done tuna, this is the time to increase the cooking time, not

Note: Cooking time should not exceed five minutes.

Spicy Scallops with Bok Choy

<u>Yield:</u> 2 servings

INGREDIENTS

Preparation Step:	Sea scallops	18ea
	Rice wine	2oz
Step one:	Marinated scallops	18ea
	Fat (peanut oil)	2tsp
	Fat (sesame seed oil)	1tsp
Step two:	Minced garlic	1tsp
	Chopped scallion	¼ cp
	Granulated sugar	a pinch
	Grated ginger root	½ tsp
Step three:	Reserved marinade	2oz
	Prepared chicken stock (bouillon)	¼ cp
	Salt	(to taste)
	Red pepper flakes	¼ tsp
	Chopped bok choy cabbage	1cp
	Prepared oyster sauce	2Tb
Step four:	Corn starch slurry (see notes)	¼ cp = 1Tb to 2oz water

Nutrition Facts

Amount per Serving
Calories 427.8
Total Fat 10.1 g
Saturated Fat 1.0 g
Polyunsaturated Fat 1.4 g
Monounsaturated Fat 4.3 g
Cholesterol 105.0 mg
Sodium 909.6 mg
Potassium 63.6 mg
Total Carbohydrate 19.7 g
Dietary Fiber 0.3 g
Sugars 9.9 g
Protein 51.7 g

METHOD

<u>Preparation step</u>: Put the scallops into the white wine and let marinate while you are arranging and preparing other ingredients.

<u>Step one</u>: Remove scallops from marinade. Strain and reserve the marinade. Combine the soy and sesame oils. In a preheated standard 14" wok, place the combined oils and over high heat, stir fry the scallops just long enough to sear them. Then remove them and set aside.

<u>Step two</u>: To the oil in the wok add the garlic, onion, granulated sugar and grated ginger root. Stir fry for thirty seconds.

<u>Step three</u>: Add the stock, reserved marinade, salt and red pepper flakes, oyster sauce and bok choy cabbage.

Step four: Using the Chan, move the food up the side of the wok and immediately add corn starch slurry to the liquids in the center of the wok and continue stirring. When slurry thickens to a sauce and is clear, return the scallops to the wok for an additional two minutes. Remove and eat.

NOTES
General:
    A-Unless a cooking time is noted, go immediately from one step to the next.

Preparation step:
    A-Marinating is a method used to tenderize and season the product before cooking.

Step one:
    A-Our object here is only to sear the natural juices into the scallops. If we caramelize the garlic and onions first, and then add the scallops, the juices from the garlic and onions will steam and we don't want that because it would tend to make the scallops tough.

Step two:
    A-Caramelize the garlic first, then the onions, then the ginger root and finally, add the sugar. This will turn into a nice little glaze.

Step three:
    A-No real cooking time is needed for the liquids in step three. There is no need for reduction of liquid here. The sauce is provided by the slurry in step four.

Step four:
    A-The corn starch slurry is made of one part corn starch to two parts liquid. The liquid chosen can be chicken stock, water, sherry, or what ever suits your taste. If unsure, use water.
    B-The slurry thickens the product within a very short period of time and is finished only when the sauce is clear. The scallops are added after the sauce clears and are heated for only two minutes. More than that will toughen the scallops.

Note: Cooking time should not exceed five minutes.

Pan Frying

Pan frying is probably the most universal or well known cooking method for fish. Pan frying takes place is a skillet or sauteuse, a skillet being a much heavier cast iron pan also called a Griswold. A sauteuse can be used for pan frying but it tends to heat the oil too quickly and allows it to cook more quickly making heat maintenance a problem. A skillet is preferable for pan frying. The cooking medium is a generous amount of oil. Some people are reluctant to cook this way because of fear of excessive fat. Some oils like canola or olive oil are unsaturated and do not pose a health threat. In fact have health benefits. But this is a cook book not a health guide, so use the oil that your taste, health concerns and pocketbook allow. As we stated before, the ethnic flavor you want to achieve will also dictate what oil you use. Oriental cooking should be done in a soy/sesame oil combination, Italian in olive oil, while the French use better and/or margarine. For true Southern or Creole cooking animal fats like lard, butter and fatback are used for flavor. Fats and oils have a lot to do with the flavor of the product being cooked.

Regardless of what fat you chose, a generous amount is required. The fat or oil in pan frying should cover about 1/3 of the product being cooked. The product being cooked is usually a fish fillet such as sole, flounder, snapper, catfish etc. The recipes below will be for a specific fish, but you can substitute any of these thin, fragile, non fatty fish you want. Other suitable fish for

Pan frying are blackfish and tile fish. Fish like blue fish, salmon and tuna are not good fish for pan frying because they already contain ample fat for flavor and cooking. If you have ever gone into a house and encountered an awful smell that made you know that someone was frying fish, that someone was probably pan frying a fatty fish.

Any fish that is to be pan fried must have a coating. This coating acts to maintain the structural integrity of the fish and also protects the flesh of the fish from absorbing too much of the fat or oil in which it is being fried. The choice of oil can be dictated by the ethnic flavoring desired by the cook, so too with the coating. Italians tend to pan fry everything in flavored bread crumbs. Many Oriental styles use a coating of rice flour. Southern cooking usually requires the use of a coating of corn meal. The French usually dust the product to be fried in plain flour. If you want to achieve a particular ethnic authenticity in your cooking, you should use the traditional oils and coatings. For the recipes in our chapter on stir frying, we included a preparation step to talk about the marinade. In this chapter the preparation step will be devoted to standard procedures for breading and coating and will be called "coating procedure". There are a number of different procedures, but the general procedure is flour first, egg wash second, bread crumbs third. This standard breading procedure tends to be foolproof.

Why do these ethnic cuisines use these particular oils and coatings? It is because, that's what was available to the traditional cook in those areas. In America, if you walk into an ethnic household, you are likely to find only the ingredients used in their national cuisine. I remember as a kid being invited by Bruce's mother Marsha, to have lunch with him. She always tried to make me feel at home by serving a side order of pasta to go along with the gefilte fish and horseradish. The thought was nice but when I got the spaghetti, Marsha would ask "so, do you want this with ketchup or butter?" In today's cosmopolitan America, most or all major ethnic ingredients are readily available in most parts of the county. Therefore, you are not precluded from mixing and matching. Cook a piece of fish coated in corn meal in some soy/sesame oil. It's okay. You are not restricted by what is on the pages of a recipe book. Experiment! (Just don't serve anything with pasta and ketchup. (Sorry Marsha!)

The actual pan frying procedure requires putting the needed amount of oil in a cold pan then heating it to a temperature just below its smoking point. You can tell when you have reached this point by looking for slight movement in the oil or a bluish glaze on the surface of the oil. You can also take **a drop** of water and place it in the oil. If it crackles, the oil should be about right. (Use extreme caution. The oil at this temperature can badly burn you so "a drop of water" means just a drop of water.) When the oil has reached its proper temperature, the coated fish is added to the oil. Once again, remember to use enough oil to allow the fish to move freely in the pan (usually this means enough oil to cover 1/3 of the fish) and use a pan large enough to allow the fish to be turned over easily. First pan fry on one side until the fish is golden brown. If the product is too dark, the heat is too high and the product is being burned. If the fish is not simmering in the oil, the oil is not hot enough and the fish will quickly become soggy and saturated with oil and so becomes neither tasty nor healthy. Then turn the fish and cook the other side 'til golden brown. The complete cooking process for a thin piece of fish should take no more than three minutes. A piece of fish to be pan fried should be no more than 1/2" at its thickest. If you pan fry a piece of fish thicker than 1/2", do not add frying time. You will burn the coating. If you need a thicker piece of fish to be cooked completely, put it in an oven at 350 degrees for an additional three to five minutes. The whole purpose here is to effect the conduction of the heat from the pan to the oil, and the oil to the coating.

After the fish is removed from the oil, it should be drained of excess fat or oil by placing it on a brown paper bag or other absorbent surface like a paper towel. Serve and eat.

The following recipes are of ethnic origin. Make not of the usage of the oils and coatings. Then make up your own recipes using different fishes, oils and coatings.

Fillet of Sole Oreganata

<u>Yield:</u> 2 servings

INGREDIENTS

Coating procedure:	Flour	¼ cp/2oz
	Egg wash (whole beaten egg)	1 egg
	Italian flavored bread crumbs	¼ cp
	Fillet of Sole	4 pc (3oz ea)
Step one:	Breaded Sole	4 pieces
	Fat (Olive oil)	¼ cp/2oz
Step two (garnish):	Minced garlic	½ tsp
	Coarsely chopped red onion	2Tb
	Chopped tomato	¼ cp
	Oregano	½ tsp
	Balsamic vinegar	2Tb
	Salt and Pepper	to taste

Nutrition Facts
Amount per Serving
Calories 313.6
Total Fat 10.8 g
Saturated Fat 1.6 g
Polyunsaturated Fat 1.2 g
Monounsaturated Fat 4.4 g
Cholesterol 163.2 mg
Sodium 305.2 mg
Potassium 107.1 mg
Total Carbohydrate 17.7 g
Dietary Fiber 1.1 g
Sugars 2.5 g
Protein 49.6 g

METHOD

<u>Coating procedure:</u> Put the flour, the egg wash and the bread crumbs in separate bowls. Dip each piece of fish first in the flour, then in the egg wash, then in the bread crumbs and set aside.

<u>Step one:</u> Heat the olive oil in a pan large enough to accommodate two pieces of fish with some room to spare, to just below the smoking point. Place two pieces of coated fish in the pan. Fry until golden brown on each side. Remove and drain. Place in warm spot or in a 200 degree oven to keep fish hot. Repeat procedure with other two pieces of fish.

<u>Step two:</u> Combine the garlic, onions, tomato and oregano. Use as garnish for the top of the cooked fish. Salt and pepper to taste, sprinkle with balsamic vinegar. That's Italian! You could even serve this dish cold the day after on a bed of greens, 'Day Old Sole'.

NOTES

<u>Coating procedure:</u>
   A-Make sure the bowls are large enough for the fish to slosh around in.
   B-Just dust the fish with the flour. Remove excess flour from fish by patting.
   C-Make sure you coat the fish in the proper order (i.e. flour, egg wash, bread crumbs) this is standard coating procedure.

<u>Step one:</u>
   A-Careful not to break the fish. The pan needed to be large enough to allow the easy movement and turning of the fish.

B-If you have a pan large enough to do all four pieces of fish at the same time, that's great. You will need to increase the amount of oil concomitantly. You can also eliminate the storing of the fish in a 200 degree oven.

C-When placing the fish in the pan and when turning it over make sure to lay the fish down and away from you. If you lay it down towards you, you run the risk of burning yourself with any oil that splashes.

<u>Step two</u>:

A-This is used as a garnish for color and taste enhancement. The balsamic vinegar is a typical Italian usage for fried foods. If you want to go "abondanza" add some grated parmesan cheese as well.

Note: Cooking time should not exceed five minutes. The caloric content will be considerably less than disclosed due to the retention and not the consumption of all the cooking oil. One cup of oil has 1,910 calories.

Catfish with Tartar Sauce

<u>Yield:</u> 2 servings

INGREDIENTS

Coating procedure:	AP flour	¼ cp
	Egg wash (whole beaten egg)	1 egg
	Yellow corn meal	¼ cp
	Fillet of Catfish	2pc (4-6 oz ea)
Step one:	Breaded Catfish	2 pieces
	Fat (Lard or vegetable oil)	¼ cp/2oz
Step two (garnish):	Light mayonnaise	¼ cp
	Coarsely chopped onion	2Tb
	Sweet pickle relish	2Tb
	Worcestershire Sauce	2Tb
	Lemon juice	1Tb
	Salt and Pepper	(to taste)

Nutrition Facts

Amount per Serving
Calories 441.6
Total Fat 17.1 g
Saturated Fat 2.5 g
Polyunsaturated Fat 4.9 g
Monounsaturated Fat 6.2 g
Cholesterol 171.0 mg
Sodium 639.2 mg
Potassium 75.9 mg
Total Carbohydrate 35.4 g
Dietary Fiber 1.2 g
Sugars 6.0 g
Protein 49.9 g

METHOD

<u>Coating procedure</u>: Put the flour, the egg wash and the corn meal in separate bowls. Dip each piece of fish first in the flour, then in the egg wash, then in the corn meal and set aside.

<u>Step one</u>: Heat the lard or oil in a pan large enough to accommodate one piece of fish with some room to spare. Heat the melted oil to just below the smoking point. Place coated fish, one piece at a time, in the pan. Fry until golden brown on each side. Remove and drain. Place in warm spot or in a 200 degree oven to keep fish hot. Repeat procedure with other piece of fish. Serve with tartar sauce, corn bread and collards if y'all want to be traditional.

<u>Step two</u>: Combine the mayonnaise, relish, chopped onions, Worcestershire Sauce, lemon juice, salt and pepper in a small bowl and you have just made tartar sauce. Or you can buy it in a jar.

NOTES

<u>Coating procedure:</u>
    A-Make sure the bowls are large enough for the fish to slosh around in.
    B-Just dust the fish with the flour. Remove excess flour from fish by patting.
    C-Make sure you coat the fish in the proper order (i.e. flour, egg wash, corn meal) is standard coating procedure.

Step one:
    A-Careful not to break the fish. The pan needs to be large enough to allow the easy movement and turning of the fish.

B-If you have a pan large enough to do both pieces of fish at the same time, that's great. You will need to increase the amount of oil proportionately. You can also eliminate storing the fish in a 200 degree oven.

C-When placing the fish in the pan and when turning it over make sure to lay the fish down away from you. If you lay it down towards you, you run the risk of burning yourself with any oil that splashes.

Step two:

A-This is tartar sauce. You can make it by combining mayonnaise and pickle relish in equal parts or buy it in a grocery store.

Note: Cooking time should not exceed five minutes. The caloric content will be considerably less than disclosed due to the retention and not the consumption of all the cooking oil. One cup of oil has 1,910 calories.

Flounder Françoise with Tarragon

<u>Yield:</u> 2 servings

INGREDIENTS

Coating procedure:	Flour	¼ cp
	Egg wash (whole beaten egg)	1 egg
	Fillet of Flounder	2 pc (4-6 oz each)
Step one:	Coated Flounder	2 pc
	Butter	2 oz
	Olive oil	1oz
Step two:	(Sauce) Coarsely chopped shallots	2 Tb
	Capers	1 Tb
	Flour (AP)	1 Tb
	Tarragon vinegar	1 Tb
	Chicken stock	¼ cp
	Sugar	½ tsp
	Fresh tarragon	½ tsp
	Salt and Pepper	(to taste)

Nutrition Facts

Amount per Serving
Calories 579.1
Total Fat 42.6 g
Saturated Fat 17.1 g
Polyunsaturated Fat 2.6 g
Monounsaturated Fat 17.7 g
Cholesterol 226.1 mg
Sodium 237.7 mg
Potassium 116.5 mg
Total Carbohydrate 14.2 g
Dietary Fiber 0.8 g
Sugars 1.0 g
Protein 50.0 g

METHOD

<u>Coating Procedures:</u> Place the flour and egg wash in separate bowls. Dip each piece of fish first in the flour, then in the egg wash and set aside.

<u>Step one:</u> Heat the butter and oil together in a pan large enough to accommodate one piece of fish with some room to spare; heat to just below the smoking point. Place coated fish in the pan. Fry until golden brown on each side. Remove and drain. Place in a 200 degree oven to keep fish hot. Repeat procedure with other piece of fish. Serve with tarragon sauce.

<u>Step two:</u> After frying the fish and removing it from the sauté pan, pour off most of the fat leaving only a small amount of fat in the pan. Add the shallots, capers and flour and sauté for 30 seconds. Add tarragon vinegar, sugar, fresh tarragon, chicken stock and salt and pepper to taste. Remove immediately and pour directly over cooked fish. Serve with vegetables and rice.

NOTES

<u>Coating Procedures</u>:
  A-Make sure the bowls are large enough for the fish to slosh around in.
  B-Just dust the fish with the flour. Remove excess flour from fish by patting.

C-Make sure you coat the fish in the proper order (i.e. flour then egg wash). This is standard coating procedure. In omitting the third coating found in the previous two recipes, we are using a coating method known as "Anglaze" or "English style."

Step one:

A-Careful not to break the fish. The pan needs to be large enough to allow the easy movement and turning of the fish.

B-Remember butter has a lower smoking point. Be careful to keep the butter from burning. Keep the heat regulated.

C-If you have a pan large enough to do both pieces of fish at the same time, that's great. You will need to increase the amount of butter and oil proportionately. You can also eliminate the storing of the fish in a 200 degree oven.

D-When placing the fish in the pan and when turning it over make sure to lay the fish down away from you. If you lay it down towards you, you run the risk of burning yourself with any melted butter that splashes.

Step two:

A-By the removal of the butter and oil and adding the ingredients to the pan, you have created a tarragon sauce using the sauté method.

B-If in the final few seconds, you find your sauce to be too thick or "goopy", just add a little more chicken stock.

Note: Cooking time should not exceed five minutes. The caloric content will be considerably less than disclosed due to the retention and not the consumption of all the cooking oil. One cup of oil has 1,910 calories.

Deep Frying

Deep frying has a bad reputation 'vies a vies' health concerns. Much of this concern is, in my opinion, unfounded. Here's why: If the oil is fresh and very hot, it is not absorbed into the product easily. Cooking times tend to be very fast, so there is little time for the absorption of the oils into the product. The coating procedure acts as insulation against the oil, so the product is actually steamed by its own juices rather than by the oil itself. The oil is almost always going to be a vegetable oil all of which are cholesterol free.

However, deep frying is a method I have a great reluctance to discuss because it can be a very dangerous procedure; if improper equipment is used and handled carelessly. Remember that boiling oil (350 degrees) is a heck of a lot hotter than boiling water (212 degrees Fahrenheit), and when in contact with skin tends to stick to it rather than roll off it or evaporate. Oil burns are extremely painful. Burning yourself with boiling oil is an experience to be missed. I speak from experience. There are, however, so many great fish recipes which are perfect for this method. It is a quick and easy procedure and because the product is cooked totally submersed in oil it tends to be very tasty.

Safety can be assured with the use of proper equipment. A spaghetti pot full of boiling oil set on top of a range is not a good way to deep fry. It is unstable and the heat is difficult to regulate. Buy a deep frying appliance which is electric, so it can be used far away from open flames, has a basket for easy handling, and a thermostat for proper oil heat maintenance. **350 degrees Fahrenheit is the only temperature for boiling cooking oil.** Cooler oil results in a soggy product. Hotter oil results in a burnt product. It's that simple, so use an appliance with a thermostat.

As a final safety tip, make sure no water is dropped into boiling oil. It will explode violently and cause severe burns.

The amount of oil that is used in a deep fryer is significant. A half gallon to a gallon of oil is usually required. The product needs to be totally submerged in oil. This sounds really expensive, but in deep frying, the oil is saved, strained and reused. One attractive aspect to this is that the oils tend to take on flavors from the products being cooked in them. One of my best customers, who also happens to be the amanuensis for this cookbook, loves my French fries when I cook them in oil previously used to cook fish.

In my opinion, the cooking time is determined by sight alone. When the product is golden brown, it's done. All products that are deep fried are "silver dollar" sized or smaller such as shrimp, scallops and chunks of cod or monkfish. Thin fish like flounder are better off being pan fried. Oily fish such as bluefish or salmon should be broiled or poached.

As in pan frying, coating is necessary to protect the product from being overcooked and absorbing too much oil. Coating also adds extra flavor. There are many different coating procedures. Beer batters and tempura are the most popular coatings. Both are discussed below.

English Style Fish and Chips

<u>Yield:</u> 2 servings
INGREDIENTS

Preparation step:	Frying oil (soy, canola or corn oil)	1cp/8oz
Coating procedure:	Flour	¼ cp
(Batter)	Egg wash (whole beaten egg)	1 egg
	Paprika	½ tsp
	Sugar	½ tsp
	Baking powder	½ tsp
	Ice	½ cp
	Light beer ½ cp/4oz Scrod Fillets	2 pc (4-6oz each)
Step one:	Coated scrod	2 pc
Step two:		
(Garnish)	Balsamic vinegar	1Tb
	Deep fried Idaho potatoes	8oz

Nutrition Facts

Amount per Serving
Calories 521.3
Total Fat 19.4 g
Saturated Fat 2.8 g
Polyunsaturated Fat 1.6 g
Monounsaturated Fat 10.9 g
Cholesterol 163.0 mg
Sodium 216.4 mg
Potassium 556.4 mg
Total Carbohydrate 46.2 g
Dietary Fiber 2.5 g
Sugars 3.6 g
Protein 52.7 g

METHOD
<u>Preparation step</u>: Heat oil to 350 degrees F.

<u>Coating procedure</u>: Place all the ingredients except the fish into a large bowl. Stir together with a spoon until beer batter is smooth. Cut the scrod into finger-like pieces being careful not to cut your fingers into scrod-like pieces. Dip each piece individually and immediately begin frying.

<u>Step one</u>: Fry scrod one piece at a time until golden brown. Place on absorbent paper. Reserve the fish in a preheated, 200 degree oven.

<u>Step two</u>: After the last piece of fish is fried, drained and placed in the preheated oven, fry the potatoes in the same oil the fish was cooked in. Sprinkle the fish and potatoes with balsamic vinegar and serve. Serve with the rest of the six-pack of beer.

NOTES
<u>Preparation step</u>: If you are not using a regulated heating device, you need a candy thermometer to insure the oil is as close to 350 degrees F. as possible. An appliance with a thermostat is preferred.

<u>Coating procedure</u>:
   A-Make sure the bowl is large enough to accommodate all the ingredients of this classic beer batter.

B-The purpose of the ice is to keep the baking powder from reacting to the heat. The baking powder is needed to make the batter crispy and fluffy. Without the ice, the baking powder will react to the heat and exhaust itself giving you a limp and soggy batter.

C-Try to get the scrod pieces about the same size so that you get used to the proper cooking time.

D-The batter has to heavily coat the fish. If the batter is too thin, add more flour.

Step one:

A-When frying, golden brown is what we are looking for.

B-**Be careful placing the fish in the oil. Don't splatter.**

C-As the fish cooks, the batter will puff up and the fish will float. Turn the fish over once during cooking so both sides get browned.

Step two:

A-Frying the potatoes in the same oil as the fish, enhances the flavor of the fries.

B-The balsamic vinegar is traditional but optional.

Note: Cooking time for each piece of fish should not exceed forty one minute. The caloric content will be considerably less than disclosed due to the retention and not the consumption of all the cooking oil. One cup of oil has 1,910 calories.

Bang-Bang Shrimp

<u>Yield:</u> 2 servings
INGREDIENTS

Preparation step:	Soy oil	½ pt

Coating procedure:		
(Batter)	AP Flour	¼ cp
	Rice flour	¼ cp
	Egg wash (whole beaten egg)	1 egg
	Sugar	1 tsp
	Baking powder	½ tsp
	Ice	½ cp
	Sake wine	¼ cp
	Titi shrimp (Frozen)	3dz

Step one:	Battered titi shrimp	36 pc

Step two:	Mayonnaise	¼ cp
(Sauce)	Red curry paste	½ tsp
	Cayenne pepper	pinch
	Chili powder	¼ tsp
	Lime juice	1Tb
(Garnish)	Chopped scallions	1Tb

Nutrition Facts

Amount per Serving
Calories 722.9
Total Fat 29.6 g
Saturated Fat 4.3 g
Polyunsaturated Fat 7.3 g
Monounsaturated Fat 13.2 g
Cholesterol 309.8 mg
Sodium 603.3 mg
Potassium 273.2 mg
Total Carbohydrate 48.1 g
Dietary Fiber 1.5 g
Sugars 4.8 g
Protein 70.0 g

METHOD

<u>Preparation step:</u> Heat oil to 350 degrees F. It's best to use a thermometer for deep frying here. You can probably pick one up at your local hardware store.

<u>Coating procedure:</u> Place all of the batter ingredients, except the shrimp into a large bowl. Stir together with a spoon until tempura batter is smooth. Dip and immediately begin frying **six to eight pieces of shrimp at a time**.

<u>Step one:</u> Fry shrimp until golden brown. Place on absorbent paper. Keep warm in a preheated 200 degree oven.

<u>Step two:</u> After the last shrimp is fried make the sauce by combining ingredients and toss together. Garnish by topping with scallions, as Sosh would say **'Bang-Bang'**!

　　If you have batter left over, you could tempura assorted vegetables if you like. Serve with steamed rice or as an appetizer.

NOTES

<u>Preparation step</u>: If you are not using a regulated heating device, you need a candy thermometer to insure the oil is as close to 350 degrees F. as possible. An appliance with a thermostat is preferred.

<u>Coating procedure</u>:

A-Make sure the bowl is large enough to accommodate all the ingredients of this classic tempura batter.

B-The purpose of the ice is to keep the baking powder from reacting to the heat. The baking powder is needed to make the batter crispy and fluffy. Without the ice, the baking powder will react to the heat and exhaust itself giving you a limp and soggy batter.

C-The batter has to heavily coat the shrimp. If the batter is too thin, add more flour.

<u>Step one</u>:

A-When deep frying, golden brown is what we are looking for.

B-**Be careful placing the shrimp in the oil. Don't splatter.**

C-In order to hold the batter on the shrimp, drop the shrimp in the boiling oil until the batter puffs up. Then let go and cook for no more that 20 seconds.

D-Don't take shortcuts. Cook six shrimp at a time! If you try to cook more than six shrimp at a time, the puffing of the batter will mess up the shrimp and might even cause the oil to overflow and start a fire.

Note: Cooking time for six to eight pieces of shrimp should not exceed twenty to thirty seconds.

The caloric content will be considerably less than disclosed due to the retention and not the consumption of all the cooking oil. One cup of oil has 1,910 calories.

Deep Fried Scallops

Yield: 2 servings

INGREDIENTS

Preparation step:	Canola oil	½ pt
Coating procedure:	Flour (AP)	½ cp
	Egg wash (whole beaten egg)	1 egg
	Italian flavored bread crumbs	½ cp
	Sea scallops (large)	16 pc
Step one:	Coated scallops	16 pc
Step two (garnish):	Tartar sauce	¼ cp

Nutrition Facts

Amount per Serving
Calories 738.6
Total Fat 28.0 g
Saturated Fat 4.2 g
Polyunsaturated Fat 2.3 g
Monounsaturated Fat 11.2 g
Cholesterol 208.3 mg
Sodium 1,531.1 mg
Potassium 104.5 mg
Total Carbohydrate 53.7 g
Dietary Fiber 2.1 g
Sugars 13.2 g
Protein 61.3 g

METHOD

Preparation step: Heat oil to 350 degrees F.

Coating procedure: Put the flour, the egg wash and the bread crumbs in separate bowls. Dip each scallop first in the flour, then in the egg wash, then in the bread crumbs and set aside.

Step one: Fry coated scallops until golden brown **one piece at a time**. Place on absorbent paper. Keep warm in a preheated 200 degree oven.

Step two: After the last scallop is fried, drained and placed in the preheated oven, serve with tartar sauce as a dip and serve with fried potatoes.

NOTES

Preparation step: If you are not using a regulated heating device, you need a candy thermometer to insure the oil is as close to 350 degrees F. as possible. An appliance with a thermostat is preferred.

Coating procedure:
    A-You will need separate bowls for each ingredient.

Step one:
    A-When frying, golden brown is what we are looking for.
    B-Scallops are better deep fried that pan fried because they need to surrounded by the cooking medium rather than turned or flipped as in pan fried. Fragile fish and small pieces of fish are better deep fried.
    C-Don't take shortcuts. Cook one scallop at a time! If you try to cook more than one scallop at a time, the cooking time will be and immersing all the scallops at once lowers the temperature of the oil and you will wind up with soggy, oily scallops.

Note: Cooking time for each scallop should not exceed twenty seconds.

The caloric content will be considerably less than disclosed due to the retention and not the consumption of all the cooking oil. One cup of oil has 1,910 calories.

NPT Calamari (Bait)

Yield: 2 servings

INGREDIENTS

Preparation step:	Canola oil	½ pt
Marinating procedure:	Calamari (cleaned young squid)	1cp/8oz
	Granulated garlic	2oz
Coating procedure:	AP flour	½ cp
	Italian flavored bread crumbs	½ cp
	Marinated bait	1cp
Step one:	Coated calamari	1cp
Step two (garnish):	Prepared tomato sauce	1cp
	Tabasco sauce	1Tb
	Chopped fresh parsley	1Tb
	Grated parmesan cheese	2Tb

Nutrition Facts

Amount per Serving
Calories 461.8
Total Fat 17.7 g
Saturated Fat 3.4 g
Polyunsaturated Fat 2.0 g
Monounsaturated Fat 10.8 g
Cholesterol 129.3 mg
Sodium 1,465.3 mg
Potassium 489.1 mg
Total Carbohydrate 56.5 g
Dietary Fiber 5.0 g
Sugars 9.3 g
Protein 20.4 g

METHOD

Marinating procedure: Slice calamari body into thin slices. Keep tentacles whole. Sprinkle liberally with the granulated garlic. Let stand for as long as you possibly can. Twenty four hours refrigerated is not too long; if you can stand the smell from the garlic and squid combination, the longer the better and more tender it will be!

Coating procedure: Put the flour and the bread crumbs together in one bowl. Toss all the calamari a half a cup at a time in the flour/breadcrumb mixture.

Preparation step: Heat oil to 350 degrees F.

Step one: Fry the calamari a little at a time making sure the calamari is swimming freely in the oil. Remove when golden brown and drain on absorbent paper.

Step two: After the last of the calamari is fried and drained, place on serving platter. Sprinkle with garnish of parmesan and parsley. Serve with lemon wedges and a bowl of your favorite spicy tomato sauce laced with Tabasco for dipping.

NOTES

Preparation step:

If you are not using a regulated heating device, you need a candy thermometer to insure the oil is as close to 350 degrees F. as possible. An appliance with a thermostat is preferred.

Marinating procedure:

A-We're not only marinating but tenderizing. The garlic tends to tenderize the calamari and the longer the better within limits. After twenty four hours the calamari may start to turn to mush.

B-This recipe calls for frozen calamari. The frozen is easier to work with because it is pre cleaned, easier to find in the store and is much easier to slice in its frozen state. However, the true aficionado might prefer fresh calamari. If you can find it, you will need to skin, decapitate, de-beak, gut and clean it before slicing it. You can tell fresh calamari by its pink and black flecked outer skin with head and entrails in tact. Here's how to clean it: Grab its body in your left hand (to be politically correct we must note if you are a lefty, grab it in your right hand) rip off its head, pinch the back of the head with your thumb and forefinger, squeeze the back of its tentacles exposing the beak. Pinch off the beak and discard. Go back to the body and under running water (if there is no drought) open the body and sticking your finger into the cavity, scoop out all the innards. Don't be shocked if you get black ink all over the sink. Make sure the quill, entrails and ink sack are all removed. Then remove the outer layer of skin. Proceed as above. If this whole procedure turns you completely off, give it to your spouse, the fisherperson, and let him or her use it as bait.

Coating procedure:

A-In this recipe, the flour takes the place of the egg wash absorbing the marinade and the natural juices from the calamari. There is no need for egg. There is no need for separate bowls.

Step one:

A-When frying golden brown is what we are looking for.

B-Calamari is better deep fried that pan fried because it needs to surrounded by the cooking medium.

C-Don't take shortcuts. Cook one half cup at a time. If you don't, you will get calamari which is burnt on the outside and soggy on the inside. I pride myself on being in the "Calamari Hall of Fame" so please don't screw this up by trying to cook it all at once.

Note: Cooking time for each half cup of calamari should not exceed two to three minutes.
The caloric content will be considerably less than disclosed due to the retention and not the consumption of all the cooking oil. One cup of oil has 1,910 calories.

Poaching/ Steaming

Poaching and steaming are both methods that are used when you are looking for lighter fare with light sauces, cold sauces or no sauces at all. Fresh herbs and spices take a much larger role in these methods. It is from them that the flavor of poached and steamed dishes is derived. Poaching and steaming are excellent methods for warm weather cooking because the products lend themselves easily to being chilled. Summer buffets and brunches are ideal settings for steamed and poached foods. These methods can be utilized to cook large pieces of fish like a whole fillet of salmon or small food bits such as shrimp for a shrimp cocktail. Poaching usually takes place in a flavored cooking medium known in the trade as "Court bouillon" and is associated strongly with French cuisine. Steaming, on the other hand, is more strongly associated with Oriental cookery as food is placed on a rack above the cooking medium.

When seafood is poached in a flavored liquid, it receives from that liquid, a light flavoring. For instance, a very herbaceous broth containing strong herbs like basil or bay leaf will impart that flavoring to the fish.

When seafood is steamed, the same effect is created but on a milder level. Steaming over wines like sake and plum wine will subtly flavor the flesh of the fish.

One of the most beneficial aspects to both these methods is that there is no fat involved in the cooking medium. When I am visited by customers with a limited diet, I opt for steaming or poaching. These methods which are sometimes considered to produce a bland product can actually be very tasty if proper herbs and spices are used.

The cooking mediums used in poaching and steaming could be store-bought chicken or fish bouillon or a "court bouillon" can be made at home which is simply a herb flavored liquid to cook something in. Once it has been used to cook something in and has acquired the flavor from that something, you have the makings of a good soup stock. Waste not, want not! See the chapter on stocks for the Court Bouillon recipe.

Wine is extremely important in these cooking processes because its acidic properties facilitate the necessary congealing of the proteins in the fish thus insuring against flaking and breaking.

Poaching is similar to deep frying only in the sense that the product is totally immersed in a hot liquid. However whereas deep frying takes place in a boiling oil, poaching takes place in a water based medium. The liquid is brought to a boil, the fish is added and the temperature of the liquid must be dropped back immediately to a simmer. If the fish is allowed to stay in an aggressively boiling medium it will break apart. If shellfish is so treated it will overcook and toughen. Maintaining a simmer is critical.

On the other hand, in steaming the medium needs to boil in order to produce the vapors needed to cook the product on the rack above the liquid. This rack, mentioned in the preceding text, is usually a bamboo steamer which fits over a pot. A set of these racks can be employed to cook the rice and the vegetables at the same time and over the same source as the fish.

Fatty fish such as salmon, mackerel and bluefish are well suited for poaching and steaming because they contain their own fats and fat flavors thus don't require the enhancement of a boiling oil or fat.

Poached Fillet of Salmon chilled with a Yogurt Cucumber Dill Sauce

Yield: 2 servings
INGREDIENTS

Step one:	Court bouillon (see recipe in text)	1pt
	Salmon fillet	2pc (6-8oz ea)

Step two:		
(Sauce)	Plain yogurt	½ cp
	Peeled, seeded and chopped cucumber	1sm
	Fresh dill	1tsp
	Sugar	½ tsp
	Salt and pepper	(to taste)

Nutrition Facts

Amount per Serving
Calories 389.7
Total Fat 15.5 g
Saturated Fat 2.8 g
Polyunsaturated Fat 5.9 g
Monounsaturated Fat 5.1 g
Cholesterol 129.1 mg
Sodium 713.1 mg
Potassium 1,360.1 mg
Total Carbohydrate 11.1 g
Dietary Fiber 0.6 g
Sugars 10.5 g
Protein 48.7 g

METHOD

Step one: In a large sauté pan (12" or more), bring the court bouillon to a boil over high heat and place the salmon in it. Immediately reduce the liquid to a simmer. Cook for 2-3 minutes. Remove and place in the refrigerator.

Step two: Combine the yogurt, the chopped cucumber, dill, sugar, salt and pepper in a bowl and refrigerate. When the salmon is chilled, place on a bed of field greens or 'salade de choix' (fancy, made up term for any kind of lettuce your little heart desires). Spoon the sauce over the fish and serve to the bridge club for luncheon.

NOTES

Step one:

   A-Make sure the salmon is covered by the liquid. If it is not possible to do so, the salmon will have to be **gently** turned over once during poaching.

   B-In this recipe, we are looking for the gelatinization of the proteins in the fish. We know the fish is done when we can observe little striations of fat appear on the surface of the salmon.

   C-Using a larger piece of salmon will require a few more minutes cooking time.

   Step two:

   A-The longer you allow the product to remain in the refrigerator, the better the marinating process will be and the more flavorful the sauce will be.

Note: Preparation and cooking time should take less than fifteen minutes.

Poached Sea Scallops in Port Wine with Cinnamon

Yield: 2 servings
INGREDIENTS

Step one:	Court bouillon (see recipe in text)	1 pt
	Port wine	½ cp
	Cinnamon sticks	2 sticks
	Sea scallops	1 lb (16 ea)

Step two:	Reserved court bouillon	1 cp
	Port wine	½ cp
	Sugar	1 Tb
	Ground cloves	¼ tsp
	Corn starch slurry (see notes)	¼ cp

Nutrition Facts

Amount per Serving
Calories 390.7
Total Fat 2.5 g
Saturated Fat 0.0 g
Polyunsaturated Fat 0.0 g
Monounsaturated Fat 0.0 g
Cholesterol 87.5 mg
Sodium 970.6 mg
Potassium 0.2 mg
Total Carbohydrate 18.9 g
Dietary Fiber 0.1 g
Sugars 12.6 g
Protein 42.5 g

METHOD

Step one: In a large sauté pan (12" or more), bring the court bouillon and port wine to a boil over high heat and place the scallops in it. Immediately reduce the liquid to a simmer. Cook for 2-3 minutes. Stir occasionally, turning the scallops. Remove when tender and reserve. Strain and then reserve the court bouillon.

Step two: Combine all the ingredients listed in step two except for the slurry and bring to a boil. Add slurry to thicken. Return scallops and cinnamon sticks for 30 seconds, remove and serve with a garnish of chilled pickled beets and greens, just for effect. Spoon the thickened poaching liquid over the scallops and serve chilled.

NOTES

Step one:
   A-Make sure the scallops are covered by the liquid. If it is not possible to do so, they will have to be gently turned over once during the process.
   B-The addition of the port wine will lightly tint the scallops and enhance their flavor.

Step two:
   A-The proper straining of the liquid will eliminate sediments.
   B-The infusion of the remaining ingredients adds flavor and enhances the effect of the court bouillon releasing even more flavor when the product is thickened.
   C-The beets provide a nice background, flavor and color contrast to the dish.
   D-The cinnamon sticks are for flavor and garnish. Don't attempt to eat them whole.

Note: From step one to step two should take less than ten minutes.

Steamed Sea Bass on a bed of Leeks with Enoki Mushrooms and Sesame Seeds

Yield: 2 servings
INGREDIENTS

Preparation Step: (Marinade)	Sea bass fillets	2 (4-6 oz ea)
	Dry sherry	2 oz (2 shots)
	Sesame seed oil	½ oz
	Soy sauce	½ oz
	Chopped garlic	½ tsp
	Chopped scallions	1 Tb
	Chopped red pepper	½ cp
	Red pepper flakes	(a pinch)
	Sugar	½ tsp
Step one:	Court bouillon (see recipe in text)	1 pt
	Washed julienne leek	1 stalk
	Marinated bass	2 pc
	Enoki mushrooms	½ cp
	Sesame seeds	(a pinch)

Nutrition Facts

Amount per Serving
Calories 471.5
Total Fat 13.5 g
Saturated Fat 2.3 g
Polyunsaturated Fat 5.3 g
Monounsaturated Fat 4.3 g
Cholesterol 90.1 mg
Sodium 1,179.4 mg
Potassium 692.2 mg
Total Carbohydrate 19.9 g
Dietary Fiber 3.4 g
Sugars 9.5 g
Protein 43.4 g

METHOD

Preparation step: Place the fish in a marinade made of all the other ingredients listed in step one. Let fish marinade for one to two hours.

Step one: Place court bouillon in a sauce pot that will accommodate whatever steaming baskets you are using (i.e.—bamboo steamers) to create a steaming device. In the basket place the julienne leeks and the marinated bass on top of the leeks. Pour the marinade gently over the fish. Place mushrooms atop the fish and sprinkle with sesame seeds. Cover and bring the sauce pot to a boil with basket, reduce to a simmer. Fish is done when fish flakes to the fork and leeks are tender. Spoon a bit of the court bouillon on a plate and place the fish and leeks in the liquid. Serve hot and eat.

NOTES

Step one:
A-The purpose of the marinade is to enhance the flavor of the steamed fish. If you are on a diet which precludes eating some of the ingredients in the marinade, do without it. The leeks and the court bouillon will provide some flavoring even without a marinade. The whole idea is to find a balance between the beneficial but bland aspects of steaming and a flavorful dish.

Step two:
A-Make sure the steamers are suspended above the liquid, not immersed in it. We are steaming the product, not boiling or poaching it.
B-Make sure the product is covered to insure complete cooking of the fish.

Note: From step one to step two should take less than seven minutes.

Steamed Lobster with Vanilla Butter Sauce

<u>Yield:</u> 2 servings

INGREDIENTS

Step one:	Court bouillon (see recipe)	1pt
	Live lobster	2 (1¼ lb ea)
		<u>(12oz yield)</u>
Step two: (Sauce)	White wine	½ cp
	Vanilla bean	1ea
	Fish fumet	1cp
	Chopped shallots	2Tb
	Black peppercorns (whole)	1tsp
	Sugar	½ tsp
	Butter	¼ lb

Nutrition Facts

Amount per Serving
Calories 456.4
Total Fat 25.0
Saturated Fat 14.8 g
Polyunsaturated Fat 1.2 g
Monounsaturated Fat 7.2 g
Cholesterol 185.5 mg
Sodium 1,404.8 mg
Potassium 686.4 mg
Total Carbohydrate 9.4 g
Dietary Fiber 0.0 g
Sugars 5.1 g
Protein 38.1 g

METHOD

<u>Step one</u>: Place court bouillon in a pot whose size will accommodate whatever steaming baskets you are using, (bamboo steamers). In the basket place the lobsters. Cover and bring pot to a boil. Steam for fifteen to twenty minutes or until lobsters are done.

<u>Step two</u>: In a sauté pan place everything in step two except the butter. Bring to a boil and reduce the liquid until dry. Remove pan from heat. Stir in the butter slowly, piece by piece until all is melted, making sure that the fat does not separate. Strain through a fine sieve and serve with the steamed lobster.

NOTES

<u>Step one</u>:

A-The lobster is cooked when it is a bright red, the tail is curled in tightly against the body and by taking the lobster in one hand, turning it over and pulling back the tail, looking into the shell and seeing the meat. If the liquids in the cavity are bubbling, it is a good indicator that the lobster in finished. Another method is to split the back of the lobster and inspect the cavity. If the tamale and roe are not cooked, the meat is probably not either.

B-Distinguish the gender of a lobster without finding the roe, go to the tail. A very slender tail with very pointy nubs on the bottom indicates a male. A wider tail with hair like flippers on the bottom indicates a female.

C-Another method of determining the gender of a lobster is to place ones finger in the lobster tank and annoy a lobster. If **he** pinches you it's a male. If **she** pinches you, it's a female.

<u>Step two</u>:

A-This is a classical French butter sauce called a "Buerre Blanc". It can be used as an accompaniment to any steamed or poached fish or other seafood.

B-The stirring of the butter must be done piece by piece and not heated so high that the fat separates. The sauce derives its flavor from the white wine reduction and the infusion of the shallots and vanilla bean.

Note: Cooking time is 15 to 20 minutes.

Oven Poaching

Oven poaching is my personal favorite way to prepare and finish sea food. It's almost foolproof. It's quick. But, people tend to be afraid of using this method in the home oven because a very hot oven 450-500 degrees is required. Instead they tend to opt to broil the fish which is a complete no-no as far as I am concerned. (Notice that there is no "broiling" section in this cook book.) The overhead high heat which is imposed upon the fish tends to dry it and intensify the fishy flavor. Oven poaching is a method without a direct source of heat, but rather the product is enveloped in heat thus cooking the product from the outside in, in a more uniform manner.

Oven poaching is called oven poaching a liquid cooking medium is most important. This could be a court bouillon, white wine, chicken stock or fish stock. These mediums are needed to protect the fish from drying out and/or burning in the very high heat. An added attraction is that in addition to giving fish a flavor, the medium also takes on the flavor of the fish from the juices of the fish so when reduced, it makes a very tasty sauce. In any event, the product is immersed 1/3 of the way into the liquid. It is critical that the product only go 1/3 of the way into the medium and remain that way for the duration of the cooking time.

All seafood from small shrimp to large fish like trout and blue fish can be prepared in this manner. All sauces can be created in the oven as well. For my taste, fish fillets like scrod and catfish are the best suited for oven poaching.

Cajun Catfish with a Creole Sauce

Yield: 2 servings
INGREDIENTS
Preparation Step:

(Dusting spice)	Paprika	3Tb
	Cayenne pepper	½ tsp
	Red pepper flake	½ tsp
	Thyme	1tsp
	Chili powder	1tsp
	Dried basil	1tsp
	Dried parsley flakes	1tsp
	Sugar	½ tsp
	Salt	(to taste)

Step one:	Catfish	2 pc (6-8 oz)
	Vegetable oil	2tsp
	Dusting spice (from above)	(Pat to dust fish)

Step two:	Dusted catfish	2pc
(Sauce)	Peanut oil	½ oz
	AP flour	1Tb
	Beef stock	1cp
	Chopped onions	2Tb
	Chopped garlic	½ tsp
	Chopped peppers, green and red	½ cp
	Prepared tomato sauce	¼ cp

Nutrition Facts

Amount per Serving
Calories 390.2
Total Fat 20.8 g
Saturated Fat 4.1 g
Polyunsaturated Fat 3.0 g
Monounsaturated Fat 12.1 g
Cholesterol 108.8 mg
Sodium 549.6 mg
Potassium 962.7 mg
Total Carbohydrate 14.2 g
Dietary Fiber 1.5 g
Sugars 3.1 g
Protein 36.0 g

METHOD
Preparation step: In a bowl, combine all ingredients.

Step one: Rub the catfish with the oil. Dust lightly with the Cajun spices and reserve.

Step two: Pour the oil then the flour into a sauté pan with a metal handle, casserole dish, sheet pan, Pyrex dish etc. Place the fish in the pan. Add the stock, so fish is 1/3 the way into the liquid. Put onions, garlic, peppers, and tomato sauce on top of fish. Oven—poaches, at 350 degrees. Fish will be done in approximately 7-12 minutes. Vegetables should be evenly browned and stock should be reduced to a sauce. Serve with corn bread. Keep plenty of ice water or beer on the side.

NOTES

Step one:

A-The dusting powder you make is going to be a lot more than you need for just one recipe. Take the dusting powder and preserve it just as you would any spice. You can simply buy a Cajun spice combination and dust the fish with that instead of preparing your own. Mine is my favorite.

Step two:

A-Remember how important it is to keep fish 1/3 covered in liquid. If stock reduces to a sauce too quickly, simply add stock during the cooking process. Conversely, it there is too much stock when the fish is finished, remove the fish and reduce the stock on top of the stove to finish the sauce. Knowing how your oven cooks is important. A couple of failures will be worth it in order to master this best of all cooking methods.

Note: This dish should take less than fifteen minutes to cook.

Award Winning Monkfish with Sauerkraut and Caraway (NYS Seafood Challenge)

Yield: 2 servings
INGREDIENTS
Preparation Step:

(Marinade)	Monkfish fillet	2 pc (6-8 oz)
	Oil (canola, or soy, or corn)	1Tb
	Worcestershire sauce	2Tb
	Chopped garlic	1tsp
	Chopped onion	2Tb
	Salt and pepper	(to taste)
Step one:	Olive oil	2tsp
	Sugar	2Tb
	Chopped garlic	½ tsp
	Chopped onions	2Tb
	Caraway seed	1tsp
	Drained sauerkraut	1cp
	Prepared tomato sauce	¼ cp
Step two:	Marinated monkfish (sliced into)	8ea/ pc
	Beef stock	1cp

Nutrition Facts

Amount per Serving
Calories 451.2
Total Fat 21.0 g
Saturated Fat 4.1 g
Polyunsaturated Fat 3.1 g
Monounsaturated Fat 12.2 g
Cholesterol 108.8 mg
Sodium 1,248.4 mg
Potassium 1,031.7 mg
Total Carbohydrate 29.4 g
Dietary Fiber 3.0 g
Sugars 17.9 g
Protein 36.5 g

METHOD

Preparation step: In a bowl, combine all ingredients. Place monkfish in marinade and refrigerate for four hours or more.

Step one: In a sauté pan large enough to accommodate the fish, sauté the sugar, onions, garlic and caraway seeds in the oil. Put the sauerkraut and the tomato sauce in the pan. Sauté and stir for one minute.

Step two: Place the fish in the pan on top of the sauerkraut. Add the stock so the fish is 1/3 the way into the liquid. Oven—poaches, at 350 degrees. Fish will be done in approximately 10-15 minutes. Sauerkraut and fish should be evenly browned and stock should be reduced to a sauce. Serve with roasted potatoes.

NOTES

<u>Preparation step</u>:

A-Marinating the monkfish imparts a flavor to this otherwise bland fish, the longer the better, up to twenty four hours is ok.

<u>Step one</u>:

A-What we are doing here is making an ethnic dish, Polish German in origin called Kaputzca. I'm sure your moms made it with pork chops when you were a kid. The monkfish was my idea.

<u>Step two</u>:

A-Remember how important it is to keep fish 1/3 covered in liquid. If stock reduces to a sauce too quickly, simply add stock during the cooking process. Conversely, if there is too much stock when the fish is finished, remove the fish and reduce the stock on top of the stove to finish the sauce.

B-Monkfish is a good but underutilized fish. It is sometimes called "poor man's lobster." The French call it "lotte". A traditional version is with mustard and herbs. This will be the next recipe but we will be using scrod.

Note: To cook this dish will take less than fifteen minutes.

Scrod with Mustard and Herbs

Yield: 2 servings

INGREDIENTS

		Nutrition Facts
		Amount per Serving

Step one:

Scrod fillets	2pc (6-8 oz)	
Salt and pepper	(to taste)	
Prepared Dijon style mustard	2Tb	
Sugar	1tsp	
Chopped garlic	½ tsp	
Chopped onions	2Tb	
Thin sliced tomato	4pc	
Seasoned bread crumbs	4Tb	
Olive oil	2tsp	

Step two:

Prepared scrod fillets	2pc
Chicken stock	1cp
White wine	2oz

Nutrition Facts

Amount per Serving
Calories 486.2
Total Fat 19.8 g
Saturated Fat 4.1 g
Polyunsaturated Fat 3.4 g
Monounsaturated Fat 10.8 g
Cholesterol 109.1 mg
Sodium 1,244.6 mg
Potassium 884.5 mg
Total Carbohydrate 27.5 g
Dietary Fiber 2.1 g
Sugars 5.9 g
Protein 39.0 g

METHOD

Step one: In a sauté pan large enough to accommodate them, place the fish, seasoned with salt, pepper and sugar. Spread the mustard over the fish. Next spread the garlic and onions. Then place the tomato garnish atop the garlic and onions and sprinkle the bread crumbs on that. Pour on the olive oil.

Step two: Add the stock and wine so the fish is 1/3 the way into the liquid. Oven—poaches at 350 degrees. Fish will be done in approximately 7-12 minutes. Breadcrumbs should be browned and the sauce should have thick consistency, like gravy. Serve with escalloped potatoes.

NOTES

Step one:

A-This is simply dressing the fish in a very simple way. Any kind of flavoring can be added to the fish. You can try peppers, shallots, scallions, herbs of any kind to change the recipe to suit your taste.

B-Any prepared herbed bread crumbs will do. You could also dice your own bread crumbs and add the herbs which you prefer.

Step two:

A-Remember how important it is to keep fish 1/3 covered in liquid. If stock reduces to a sauce too quickly, simply add stock during the cooking process. Do not add more wine for thinning the stock. Conversely, it there is too much stock when the fish is finished, remove the fish and reduce the stock on top of the stove to finish the sauce.

B-Scrod is a baby codfish which is usually found in fillet, while codfish is usually found in steaks.

Note: All steps should take less than fifteen minutes.

Roasting/Baking

Since oven poaching has now brought us off the range and into the oven, I want to talk about roasting and baking. The temperature variation in an oven will vary. There are some items we don't want to cook too quickly. Some of the items we will be cooking such as whole fish or stuffed fish are large. We want to avoid drying the outside and having a raw inside. The method of the oven poaching still applies here with regard to cooking mediums especially in the roasting end of things. In baking, we are going to cook items in a crust so there is no cooking medium. Temperatures will vary between 350 and 425 degrees Fahrenheit for cooking from the outside in. Again, keep in mind that we are using whole fish whose weight can vary from one to more than seven pounds. Cooking times vary with the size of the fish. Usually 20 minutes per pound is a good guideline. The longer an item is in the oven, the lower the temperature should be. Knowing your oven is quite important.

Not many people like to eat a fish whole. But when a fish is eaten straight off the bone, it is more flavorful and fresher. A good way to tell the freshness of a fish is to feel the outside of the body. It should be firm, not slimy and have no off odors. If you spread the belly of the fish and the meat inside appears pink and does not pull apart, it is fresh. Another way is to look at the eye. A bulging eye is an indicator of freshness; a sunken eye indicates an old fish. If you examine the gills and they are bright red, you have an excellent product. If the gills are brown or ashen, the fish is probably old.

Cooking a fish whole is an easy way to cook. You can put just about anything on it. A whole fish served on a platter family style where everyone can pick at it makes for a nice presentation. Whole fish should be eaten carefully because of bones. Fish is considered cooked when the meat flakes off the bone.

When you buy a whole fish, it usually comes gutted. If you catch your own, you will have to gut it yourself. To gut a fish, take your chef knife and slip it under its pectoral fins (those are the ones on the sides) make an incision from the top of the head, slanting downward and repeat on the other side. Once the incisions have been made, grab the head with your hand and tear the head off. All the entrails should come out with the head. Or if you prefer to leave the head on, simply slice the belly open and remove the entrails. Rinse the cavity under running water removing all debris and blood. Then, scale the fish by running the fish under water by its tail and round the back of your knife up and down the fish on both sides, taking off the scales. Now you are ready to roast or bake the fish.

Whole Red Snapper with fresh herbs and ginger

Yield: 2 servings
INGREDIENTS

Step one:	Whole red snapper gutted and cleaned	1-2 lbs
	Salt and pepper	(to taste)
	Sugar	1tsp
	Chopped garlic	½ tsp
	Sliced fresh ginger	1Tb
	Thyme	1sprig
	Tarragon	1sprig
	Sage	2 leaves
	Parsley	1sprig
Step two:	Prepared snapper	1fish
	Chicken stock	1cp
	White wine	2oz
	Soy oil	2Tb
	Sesame oil	1Tb
	AP flour	2Tb

Nutrition Facts

Amount per Serving
Calories 874.8
Total Fat 23.1 g
Saturated Fat 1.0 g
Polyunsaturated Fat 1.4 g
Monounsaturated Fat 4.3 g
Cholesterol 0.0 mg
Sodium 242.0 mg
Potassium 457.4 mg
Total Carbohydrate 39.3 g
Dietary Fiber 1.7 g
Sugars 4.1 g
Protein 104.5 g

METHOD

Step one: In a sauté pan or oven platter large enough to accommodate, place the fish, seasoned with salt, pepper and sugar. Rub the garlic in the cavity of the fish. Place the herbs and ginger in the cavity of the fish.

Step two: Add the stock and wine so the fish is 1/3 the way into the liquid. Rub the top of the fish with combined oil. Stir the flour into the liquid. Place into 375 degree preheated oven. Roast for 20-30 minutes. Fish is done when it flakes with a fork. Discard the herbs and serve fish whole on a bed of steamed rice and pour the liquid from the pan over the whole thing.

NOTES

Step one:
    A-The herbs and garlic go inside the fish so that they do not burn and turn bitter. The flavor will be imparted to the fish and infuse into the liquid below.

Step two:
    A-Remember how important it is to keep fish 1/3 covered in liquid. If stock reduces to a sauce too quickly, simply add stock during the cooking process. Do not add more wine for thinning the stock. Conversely, it there is too much stock when the fish is finished, remove the fish and reduce the stock on top of the stove to finish the sauce.
    B-Rubbing the oil on the fish keeps the skin moist, lubricated so it doesn't dry out and blister. The skin of the fish adds a very nice flavor.

Note: From step one to step two should take less than half an hour.

Trout with Potato Leek Stuffing

<u>Yield:</u> 2 servings
INGREDIENTS

Preparation step: (Stuffing)	Olive oil	2 tsp
	Chopped garlic	½ tsp
	Cleaned leeks	1stalk
	Boiled Idaho potatoes	½ cp
	Salt and pepper	(to taste)
Step one:	Cleaned trout	2pc (12-16 oz/ ea)
	Prepared stuffing	(from above)
Step two:	Stuffed trout 2pc	
	Chicken stock 1cp	
	White wine 2oz	
	Bacon strips 4pc	

Nutrition Facts

Amount per Serving
Calories 745.6
Total Fat 21.7 g
Saturated Fat 2.7 g
Polyunsaturated Fat 1.8 g
Monounsaturated Fat 5.6 g
Cholesterol 30.0 mg
Sodium 601.4 mg
Potassium 479.3 mg
Total Carbohydrate 35.5 g
Dietary Fiber 0.9 g
Sugars 2.8 g
Protein 81.4 g

METHOD

<u>Preparation step</u>: In a pot, boil the potatoes and put aside when tender. Let cool. Sauté garlic and leeks in olive oil until golden and translucent. Set aside with potatoes. Mash all the ingredients together. Season with salt and pepper and set aside.

<u>Step one</u>: Stuff he cavity of the trout with a liberal amount of the potato leek stuffing. Place on an oven ready platter.

<u>Step two</u>: Add the stock and wine so the fish is 1/3 the way into the liquid. Place bacon strips over the fish. Bake at 350 degrees for twenty minutes. Serve by spooning some of the broth over the fish. Serve with steamed broccoli.

NOTES

<u>Preparation step</u>:
    A-What we are doing here is simply making mashed potatoes. You can put sour cream, chives, bacon bits, cheese, herbs or any combination thereof in the stuffing.

<u>Step one</u>:
    A-Be sure to fill the cavity of the fish completely.
    B-Place the fish in the pan belly side down to avoid drying out.

<u>Step two</u>:
    A-Remember how important it is to keep fish 1/3 covered in liquid. If stock reduces to a sauce too quickly, simply add stock during the cooking process. Do not add more wine for thinning the stock. Conversely, it there is too much stock when the fish is finished, remove the fish and reduce the stock on top of the stove to finish the sauce.
    B-Any kind of trout can be used in this recipe.

Note: Preparing this meal should take less than half an hour.

Baked Oysters with a Spinach and Worcestershire Glaze

Yield: 2 servings
INGREDIENTS

Preparation step:	Olive oil	2tsp
(Stuffing)	Chopped garlic	½ tsp
	Cleaned spinach	1cp (cooked)
	Chopped onions	2Tb
	Worcestershire sauce	2Tb
	Salt and pepper	(to taste)
Step one:	Cleaned and opened large oysters	8ea
	Prepared filling	(from above)
	Prepared Tartar sauce	½ cp
Step two:	Prepared oysters	8ea
	Olive oil	2tsp
	Chicken stock	½ cp
	White wine	2oz
	AP flour	1Tb

Nutrition Facts

Amount per Serving
Calories 293.6
Total Fat 20.9 g
Saturated Fat 3.3 g
Polyunsaturated Fat 0.9 g
Monounsaturated Fat 4.1 g
Cholesterol 38.5 mg
Sodium 1,099.6 mg
Potassium 314.8 mg
Total Carbohydrate 17.7 g
Dietary Fiber 0.5 g
Sugars 8.0 g
Protein 6.4 g

METHOD

Preparation step: In a sauté pan, sauté the garlic and onions in the oil until golden and translucent. Add spinach and continue sautéing until spinach is limp but not overcooked. Season with salt and pepper, add the Worcestershire sauce. Set aside and let cool.

Step one: Wash and carefully open oysters by slipping a knife under the oyster meat and dislodging it from the bottom shell and letting it float therein. Discard the top shell. Place 1Tb of the spinach mixture on top of the oyster and top with 1Tb of the prepared tartar sauce.
Step two: Place the prepared oysters on a cookie sheet or shallow casserole. Pour chicken stock and wine on the pan around the oysters. Stir in the flour. Bake at 425 degrees for 5 to 7 minutes or until the tartar sauce turns golden brown. Remove oysters then pour the sauce from the bottom of the sheet over the oysters. Serve as an appetizer.

NOTES

Preparation step:
   A-Use a store bought tartar sauce. If you want to make your own just combine two parts mayonnaise to one part sweet pickle relish and you have tartar sauce.

Step one:

A-**Serious note:** Opening the oysters should be done carefully. It is very easy to stab yourself in the hand. I've had two chefs named "Lefty" already; Locate the rear of the oyster which is where the hinge is. Take a can opener (a church key, not an electric can opener) or a real oyster knife and insert the tip slowly into the hinge. Hold the oyster very firmly in your hand wrapped with a towel. Move your wrist from left to right and exerting steady pressure, the oyster should pop open. Insert a knife along the shell to dislodge the oyster. Try not to spill the juice. This takes practice. You will get good at it.

Step two:

A-Remember how important it is to keep oysters 1/3 covered in liquid. If stock reduces to a sauce too quickly, simply add stock during the cooking process. Do not add more wine for thinning the stock. Conversely, it there is too much stock when the oysters are finished, remove the fish and reduce the stock on top of the stove to finish the sauce.

B-Any kind of oyster can be used in this recipe. Prepare this recipe in season.

Note: Preparation, aside from shucking should be less than seven minutes.

Whole Baked Clams Oreganata

Yield: 2 servings
INGREDIENTS

| Preparation step: | Kosher salt | (handful) |
| | Little neck clams | 1dz |

Step one:	Seasoned bread crumbs	½ cp
	Butter	¼ cp
	Chopped garlic	2cloves
	Parsley	5sprigs
	Oregano	¼ tsp

Nutrition Facts

Amount per Serving
Calories 395.0
Total Fat 25.4 g
Saturated Fat 15.1 g
Polyunsaturated Fat 1.7 g
Monounsaturated Fat 6.4 g
Cholesterol 86.2 mg
Sodium 974.9 mg
Potassium 315.7 mg
Total Carbohydrate 23.2 g
Dietary Fiber 1.5 g
Sugars 1.7 g
Protein 14.0 g

METHOD

Preparation step: On a cookie sheet spread the kosher salt so it covers the bottom. Open the clams over a bowl so that the clam juice is not wasted. Place the clam shells containing the meat from the clams on the kosher salt in the cookie sheet.

Step one: Chop the garlic and the parsley. Add to the left over clam juice, bread crumbs and oregano. Add the butter and mix till homogenous. Place dollops of the mixture on top of each clam. Put in a 350 degree oven and bake till brown and bubbly.

NOTES

Preparation step:

    A-The kosher salt is put on the cookie sheet just to give a stable base for the clam shells so they don't tilt and spill the liquids while they cook. You can use crumpled aluminum foil just as easily, but that is a waste of aluminum.

Step one:

    A-You can substitute prepared garlic and dried parsley. You can substitute store bought chopped clams and those little aluminum shells for the real clams, but if you have the time, stick with the fresh real items. Open similarly to that of the oysters and be careful.
    B-Mixing in the butter by hand can be hard. If you have a food processor just chuck everything in it and mix. You could also melt the butter for easy mixing.
    C-If you don't like whole clams, just throw the clam meat into the food processor along with everything else and put the mixture back into the shells and bake.

Note: From step one to step two should take less than thirty minutes.

Salmon Wellington

<u>Yield:</u> 2 servings

INGREDIENTS

Preparation step:	Olive oil	2tsp
(Stuffing)	Chopped garlic	½ tsp
	Chopped onions	3Tb
	Cleaned chopped shrimp	2oz
	Chopped sea scallops	2oz
	Chopped clams in juice	2oz
	Chicken stock	½ cp
	Seasoned bread crumbs	½ cp
	Whole egg	1ea
	Salt and pepper	(to taste)
Step one:	Salmon fillet	2pc (6-8 oz ea)
	Prepared stuffing	(from above)
Step two:	Stuffed salmon fillet	2pc
	Puff pastry	2 sheets (12" X 15")
Step three:	Prepared tomato sauce	½ cp
	Tarragon	½ tsp
	Half and half cream	¼ cp

Nutrition Facts

Amount per Serving
Calories 1,993.0
Total Fat 118.0 g
Saturated Fat 19.3 g
Polyunsaturated Fat 62.1 g
Monounsaturated Fat 29.2 g
Cholesterol 288.0 mg
Sodium 1,836.1 mg
Potassium 1,878.7 mg
Total Carbohydrate 143.7 g
Dietary Fiber 6.4 g
Sugars 7.3 g
Protein 86.2 g

METHOD

<u>Preparation step</u>: Sauté the garlic and onions in the olive oil until golden brown. Add shrimp and scallops and sauté an additional minute. Add chopped clams with juice and the stock. Let it reduce down by half. <u>Remove and let cool.</u> Add bread crumbs and egg. Mix in a bowl and reserve.

<u>Step one</u>: Butterfly the salmon fillet open. Place the stuffing in the salmon. Fold the top fillet over it.

<u>Step two</u>: Cut the puff pastry sheet into two parts. Place each stuffed salmon fillet on top of a piece of puff pastry and fold the pastry over. Pinch the sides and seal it. On a cookie sheet bake the salmon in a 425 degree oven on each side for 10 minutes or until pastry is golden brown.

<u>Step three</u>: In a sauce pot, combine the tomato sauce, heavy cream and tarragon. Bring to a boil, lower to a simmer. Reduce to a light sauce consistency. Spoon onto a plate and place the salmon Wellington on top of it. Serve with your favorite sautéed vegetables.

NOTES

Preparation step:

A-What we are doing here is making a bread stuffing. You can vary the ingredients in this stuffing to meet your tastes and/or dietary needs.

B-Before you add the egg, be sure the stuffing is cool, or the egg will cook.

C-If you do not use this stuffing right away, be sure to refrigerate it.

Step one:

A-Butter flying is slicing the salmon fillet open <u>but not all the way through</u>. It's kind of like pocket pita bread, with which to hold a stuffing. You need a very sharp knife. Don't cut yourself.

Step two:

A-You can buy puff pastry in the frozen food department of your local store. It is usually in sheet form.

B-When baking the puff pastry, the heat temperature is important. Puff pastry can burn easily. If one side browns too quickly, turn the salmon over and continue to bake.

Step three:

A-The sauce in this recipe is a suggestion. Any type of Hollandaise or Buerre Blanc is as acceptable as the sauce in this recipe.

Note: From step one to step three should take less than half an hour. The preparation work will take at least a half hour.

Grilling

Grilling is traditionally reserved for the summer. If you are lucky enough to have an indoor barbecue, you can do it year round. Grilling may be the only cooking method in which the source of heat (in this case wood or charcoal) actually imparts a flavor to the meal. One can grill over mesquite, hickory, cedar, apple wood, oak each of which imparts its own special woody essence. Accompanied by a nice glass of wine you can have a sweet little meal.

This method of cooking can be from start to finish. You can also cook all the courses over the same fire, the potatoes, the vegetables and even hot desserts.

Grilling is also a very healthy method of eating too because no fats are necessary. The fatty fishes such as salmon, swordfish, shark, tuna, bluefish, and mackerel are excellent for grilling. Monkfish and halibut, although not as fatty as the aforementioned, are also excellent for grilling because they can be cut into thick steaks. Shrimp, scallops and lobster can also be grilled, but with these smaller items, cooking times have to be regulated carefully. A favorite way of grilling is a kebob of seafood and vegetables.

As a rule, marinating is an important aspect of grilling. It helps to flavor the fish and the oils in the marinade help keep the fish from sticking to your grill and desiccating. Fatty fish do not really require a marinade.

Determining the doneness of the fish depends upon the thickness of the cut. For obvious reasons, a thick piece of fish is going to take longer than a piece of shrimp. The sure way of telling if a fatty piece of fish is finished is grilling on one side and when the fat striations are forced through on onto the top of the fish. This is most true of salmon. At that time, flip the fish and quickly complete it. You now have a meal flavored with a marinade and wood smoke. In my restaurant, I like to grill. It's my second favorite type of cooking. Hey, you can watch me grilling on 'You Tube' under 'Chefs Diet' educational series, exciting isn't it!

Grilled Halibut in Red Wine with Roasted Shallots

<u>Yield:</u> 2 servings
INGREDIENTS

Preparation step: (Marinade)	Olive oil	2 tsp
	Chopped garlic	½ tsp
	Small whole shallots peeled	12 ea (small)
	Red wine	¼ cp
	Fresh thyme	1sprig
	Bay leaf	2 leaves
	Sugar	1tsp
	Salt and pepper	(to taste)
Step one:	Halibut steaks 1" thick	2 pc (6-8 oz)
	Prepared marinade	(from above)
Step two:	Wood shavings	1 big handful
	Marinated halibut steaks	2 pc

Nutrition Facts

Amount per Serving
Calories 356.2
Total Fat 9.6 g
Saturated Fat 1.3 g
Polyunsaturated Fat 2.0 g
Monounsaturated Fat 5.0 g
Cholesterol 69.7 mg
Sodium 125.8 mg
Potassium 1,222.6 mg
Total Carbohydrate 13.4 g
Dietary Fiber 0.0 g
Sugars 2.3 g
Protein 47.0 g

METHOD

<u>Preparation step</u>: Combine all the ingredients in a marinade tray.

<u>Step one</u>: Put the halibut steaks in the marinade and let marinate for at least four hours.

<u>Step two</u>: Stoke your fire. Once the fire becomes a bed of brightly glowing coals, place the wood chips on the coals. Once the new flames die down, place the marinated fish. Remove the shallots from the marinade and place around the fish. Cook on one side for 3-5 minutes over a low flame then flip fish and cook for an additional 1-3 minutes. While fish is cooking, rotate the shallots.

NOTES

<u>Preparation step</u>:

A-What we are doing here is making a wine marinade. You can make any kind of marinade you want. This one is American. You can go Asian with teriyaki or English with beer too. It's up to you.

B-I wrote the word "small" next to shallots twice. Don't use big ones. They won't finish cooking in time.

<u>Step one</u>:

A-Halibut is like a large flounder. It's a flat fish usually cut into steaks. It is a very mild fish and I think it needs a strong marinade to give it flavor.

Step two:

A-Remember that this is not a fatty fish, so look for juices being force to the top as a signal it is time to flip the fish. Be gentle in prying the fish off the grill. It will tend to stick and need some coaxing, best to use a release spray on the grill first.

B-I chose oak wood to burn over. You can choose any smoky wood as your fuel. We are trying to get the wood to smoke and not completely burn away. Some people soak chips in water in order to prolong the burning process. If the chips still burn too fast, add some more. What is wanted is a nice steady stream of smoke.

C-If you see the fish is drying out and over cooking; you can baste the fish or rub the fish with the marinade, so keep it handy. Rub each side before and after turning.

Note: From step one to step two should take less than twelve minutes.

Swordfish with Eggplant Caponata

Yield: 2 servings
INGREDIENTS

Preparation step: (Marinade)	Olive oil	2 tsp
	Red wine vinegar	¼ cp
	Red wine	¼ cp
	Chopped garlic	1 tsp
	Chopped red onions	3Tb
	Chopped celery leaf	1Tb
	Small diced egg plant	½ cp
	Small diced red pepper	2Tb
	Oregano	½ tsp
	Basil	1Tb
	Raisins	1Tb
	Sugar	1Tb
	Salt and pepper	(to taste)
Step one:	Swordfish steak s 1" thick	2 pc (6-8 oz)
	Prepared marinade	(from above)
Step two:	Hickory chips	1 handful
	Marinated swordfish	2 pc

Nutrition Facts

Amount per Serving
Calories 389.7
Total Fat 13.4 g
Saturated Fat 3.0 g
Polyunsaturated Fat 2.4 g
Monounsaturated Fat 6.7 g
Cholesterol 85.0 mg
Sodium 202.1 mg
Potassium 838.1 mg
Total Carbohydrate 16.4 g
Dietary Fiber 1.3 g
Sugars 10.7 g
Protein 44.0 g

METHOD

Preparation step: Combine all ingredients in a marinade tray.

Step one: Marinate swordfish for four hours or longer.

Step two: Strain the marinade. Reserve the solid contents for later cooking. Save the oil for basting. Stoke your fire. Once the fire becomes a bed of brightly glowing coals, place the wood chips of the coals. Once the new flames die down, add the marinated fish. Cook on one side for 3-5 minutes over a low flame then flip fish and cook for an additional 1-3 minutes. While the fish is cooking, put the solid contents of the marinade that you reserved on a piece of aluminum foil and place on the grill. By the time the fish is done, the "Caponata" should be done. Serve as is.

NOTES

Preparation step:

A-What we are doing here is preparing a marinade with all the vegetables in it. This is known as a Caponata which is usually served as a cold antipasto after being cooked. Here it is being used as a hot accompaniment to the fish.

<u>Step two</u>:

A-Remember that this is a fatty fish, so look for fat striations beginning to form on the top as a signal it is time to flip the fish. Be gentle in prying the fish off the grill. It will tend to stick and need some coaxing.

B-I chose hickory wood to burn over. You can choose any smoky wood as your fuel. We are trying to get the wood to smoke and not completely burn away. Some people soak chips in water in order to prolong the burning process. If the chips still burn too fast, add some more. What is wanted is a nice steady stream of smoke.

C-If you see the fish is drying out and over cooked, you can baste the fish or rub the fish with the marinade, so keep it handy. Rub each side before and after turning.

Note: From step one to step two should take less than twelve minutes.

Barbecued Salmon with Chili Butter

<u>Yield:</u> 2 servings

INGREDIENTS

Preparation step:	Butter	¼ cp
(Compound butter)	Chili powder	½ tsp
	Cayenne pepper	(pinch)
	Sugar	1tsp
	Cumin	(pinch)
	Salt and pepper	(to taste)
	Prepared barbecue sauce	1oz
	Chopped cilantro	½ tsp
	Minced red bell pepper	1Tb
Step one:	Salmon steak 1" thick	2 pc (6-8 oz ea)
	Corn oil	2 tsp
	Salt and pepper	(to taste)
Step two:	Mesquite chips	1 handful
	Rubbed salmon steaks	2 pc

Nutrition Facts

Amount per Serving
Calories 283.9
Total Fat 27.6 g
Saturated Fat 14.9 g
Polyunsaturated Fat 1.2 g
Monounsaturated Fat 10.0 g
Cholesterol 62.2 mg
Sodium 123.3 mg
Potassium 23.8 mg
Total Carbohydrate 10.2 g
Dietary Fiber 0.2 g
Sugars 8.1 g
Protein 0.3 g

METHOD

<u>Preparation step:</u> Soften the butter in a bowl and add all the other ingredients. With a hand held mixer, whip all the ingredients together. Refrigerate. Let it harden.

<u>Step one:</u> Rub the salmon with the oil and season with salt and pepper.

<u>Step two:</u> Stoke your fire. Once the fire becomes a bed of brightly glowing coals, place the wood chips over the coals. Once the new flames die down, add the oiled fish. Cook on one side for 3-5 minutes over a low flame then flip fish and cook for an additional 1-3 minutes. Serve with a dollop of chili butter on each piece of fish.

NOTES

<u>Preparation step:</u>

A-This is a compound butter used as a sauce when it melts down. A compound butter is just whipped butter to which seasonings have been added.

<u>Step one:</u>

A-Because there is no marinade here, we need to oil the fish to keep it from sticking to the grill.

<u>Step two</u>:

A-Remember that this is a fatty fish, so look for fat striations beginning to form on the top as a signal it is time to flip the fish. Be gentle in prying the fish off the grill. It will tend to stick and need some coaxing.

B-I chose mesquite wood to burn over. This is a southwestern dish so we are using the woods indigenous to the area. You can choose any smoky wood as your fuel. We are trying to get the wood to smoke and not completely burn away. Some people soak chips in water in order to prolong the burning process. If the chips still burn too fast, add some more. What is wanted is a nice steady stream of smoke.

C-If you see the fish is drying out, you can baste the fish or rub the fish with a little bit of the compound butter, so keep it handy. Rub each side before and after turning.

Note: From step one to step two should take less than twelve minutes.

Grilled Shrimp Quesadilla

Yield: 2 Servings
INGREDIENTS

Step one:	Flour tortillas 8"	4 ea
	Grated cheddar/jack cheese	4 oz
Step two:	Olive oil	2 tsp
	Diced pineapples	½ cp
	Diced red peppers	½ cp
	Shrimp 16/20	16 oz (16 ea)
	Salt and pepper	(to taste)
Step three:	Sour cream	2 oz
(Garnish)	Chopped cilantro	2 tsp
	Diced scallions	2 tsp

Nutrition Facts

Amount per Serving
Calories 440.6
Total Fat 19.4 g
Saturated Fat 7.0 g
Polyunsaturated Fat 0.9 g
Monounsaturated Fat 4.5 g
Cholesterol 84.8 mg
Sodium 84.6 mg
Potassium 237.6 mg
Total Carbohydrate 48.5 g
Dietary Fiber 2.5 g
Sugars 6.2 g
Protein 18.7 g

METHOD

Step one: On a heated grill toast the tortillas on both sides. Let cool and reserve. Spread the cheese evenly over the tops of two individual ones.

Step two: Toss all ingredients in the olive oil and grill until fruit and vegetables are charred. Turn each shrimp making sure they are completely cooked. Cut the shrimp into pieces and spread them the pineapple and peppers over the cheese covered tortillas. Top each with the remaining tortilla (making a sandwich) and return to the grill until the cheese has completely melted.

Step three: Cut the finished tortillas into wedges and use the sour cream, cilantro and scallions as a condiment. Serve hot.

Blackening

Blackening is a fairly new method of cooking. The great Paul Prudhomme is the founding father, so to speak, of this type of cooking. Maybe he accidentally burned something once. Who knows? This form of cooking is highly associated with Cajun, Creole and other Southern fare.

I started blackening when I was in Austin, Texas. In the South I started by blackening red fish. I was probably one of the first chefs in New York to use the blackening method. Up here I used to blacken blue fish. Someone once asked me if I beat the fish up because it was a "black 'n blue fish."

A lot of people like blackened food, but most people don't know how to make a good blackened meal. Any type of fish can be blackened as long as the flesh has a firm structure. Filet of sole, cod, trout etc. are <u>not</u> suitable for blackening. Some sea food holds up well to blackening process, but has flavor which is very delicate and can get lost when blackened. Such fish include salmon, shrimp, lobster and scallops. For my taste, the optimal vehicles for blackening are fatty, fishy fish like blue fish and mackerel. Tuna, red fish, swordfish, monk fish, cat fish and shark are also excellent for blackening.

The process of blackening takes place in a "Griswold" or cast iron pan. Usually the product is dredged through a Cajun type seasoning that you can make on your own or buy. It is then placed in an extremely hot, dry and oil free skillet. Here is where the fun begins, because if you don't have one hell of an exhaust system, you will smoke out and choke everyone that is in the house. There has been many a day when I almost choked myself in a professional kitchen. For the home cook, the best thing to do is reserve this style of cooking for the summer and heat your skillet over a well stoked barbecue.

The purpose of blackening is not to cremate the fish, or even to burn the spices. It is just to get the spices to adhere to the fish. The process should not take more than thirty to forty five seconds on each side. After the fish is blackened on one side, it is turned over and blackened on the other side. But the fish is never finished in the skillet itself. The finishing of the fish is done on top of the stove or in an oven within some sort of a sauce, usually of Creole origin, in the same way we did our oven poaching. One could almost say that blackening is really oven poaching with a preliminary step.

Blackened Blue fish with 'dem' Cajun Spices

Yield: 2 servings

INGREDIENTS

Preparation step:	AP flour	¼ cp
(Blackening spice)	Chili powder	½ tsp
	Garlic powder	½ tsp
	Onion powder	½ tsp
	Cayenne pepper	(a pinch)
	Sugar	½ tsp
	Salt	(to taste)
	Thyme leaves	½ tsp
	Paprika	1Tb
	Red pepper flakes	(a pinch)
Step one:	Bluefish fillets 2 pc	(6-8 oz ea)
	Prepared blackening spices	(from above)
Step two:	Butter	2 oz
	AP flour	1Tb
	Chopped garlic	½ tsp
	Chopped onions	2Tb
	Sliced red and green peppers	¼ cp
	White wine	2 oz
	Beef stock	¼ cp
	Salt and pepper	(to taste)

Nutrition Facts

Amount per Serving
Calories 762.4
Total Fat 28.2 g
Saturated Fat 14.5 g
Polyunsaturated Fat 1.1 g
Monounsaturated Fat 6.9 g
Cholesterol 422.2 mg
Sodium 576.4 mg
Potassium 185.6 mg
Total Carbohydrate 23.4 g
Dietary Fiber 1.3 g
Sugars 1.2 g
Protein 2.6 g

METHOD

Preparation step: Combine all ingredients and reserve.

Step one: Dredge the bluefish through the blackening spices. Set aside. Heat the Griswold (skillet) over high heat for approximately three to five minutes. Place the fish into the skillet for thirty seconds, turn over and repeat. Remove fish immediately and reserve in a 200 degree oven.

Step two: In a separate sauté pan, over low heat, melt the butter, add the flour and cook until the flour turns golden brown. Add garlic, onions, peppers and sauté for three minutes. Place the fish in the pan, add stock and wine. Place in preheated 425 degree oven for three to five minutes longer. When the sauce is thick, the fish is done. Serve with corn bread.

NOTES

Preparation step:

A-We are making Phil's Cajun style spices. You can add, subtract, substitute or buy Paul Prudhomme's or some one else's prepared spices. It's a lot less expensive to do your own.

Step one:

A-Remember that the blackening pan is just the venue for blackening. It is not used again.

B-There is no need to keep the fish warm while preparing step two because it will be oven poached shortly.

Step two:

A-Do not use the same pan for step two that you used in step one. You will wind up with an extremely bitter sauce because the spices will now burn.

B-Combining the butter and the flour and cooking it is called creating a roux which is a thickening agent. In Cajun cooking, the roux you will see are the darkest roux you will see. These are called brown or golden roux. These are dark, rich gravies.

C-The finishing process in the oven is the oven poaching procedure we learned earlier in the book.

Note: From step one to step two should take less than twelve minutes.

Blackened Catfish with Sufferin' Succotash

<u>Yield:</u> 2 servings
INGREDIENTS

Preparation step:		
	AP flour	¼ cp
	Chili powder	½ tsp
	Garlic powder	½ tsp
	Onion powder	½ tsp
	Cayenne pepper	(a pinch)
	Sugar	½ tsp
	Salt	(to taste)
	Thyme leaves	½ tsp
	Paprika	1Tb
	Red pepper flakes	(a pinch)

Step one:		
	Catfish	2 pc (6-8 oz ea)
	Prepared blackening spices	(from above)

Step two:		
	Butter	2 oz
	AP flour	1Tb
	Chopped garlic	½ tsp
	Chopped onions	2Tb
	Chopped red peppers	¼ cp
	Frozen or canned Lima beans	¼ cp
	Frozen or canned Corn kernels	¼ cp
	Frozen or canned Okra slices	¼ cp
	White wine	2 oz
	Chicken stock	¼ cp
	Salt	(to taste)

Nutrition Facts

Amount per Serving
Calories 621.0
Total Fat 37.6 g
Saturated Fat 17.6 g
Polyunsaturated Fat 3.6 g
Monounsaturated Fat 14.0 g
Cholesterol 171.0 mg
Sodium 210.6 mg
Potassium 937.9 mg
Total Carbohydrate 29.4 g
Dietary Fiber 3.9 g
Sugars 2.0 g
Protein 37.1 g

METHOD
Preparation step: Combine all ingredients and reserve.

<u>Step one</u>: Dredge the catfish through the blackening spices. Set aside. Heat the Griswold (skillet) over high heat for approximately three to five minutes. Place the fish into the skillet for thirty seconds, turn over and repeat. Remove fish immediately and reserve.

<u>Step two</u>: In a separate sauté pan, over <u>low</u> heat, melt the butter, add the flour and cook until the flour turns golden brown. Add garlic, onions, peppers and sauté for three minutes. Place the fish in the pan, add stock and wine. Then add the prepared lima beans, okra, and corn kernels to the pan and place in

preheated 425 degree oven for three to five minutes longer. When the sauce is thick, the fish is done. Serve with jalapeno corn bread.

NOTES
Preparation step:

A-We are making Phil's Cajun style spices. You can add, subtract, substitute or buy Paul Prudhomme's or some one else's prepared spices. It's a lot less expensive to do your own.

Step one:

A-Remember, that the blackening pans just the venue for blackening. It is not used again until the pan is cleaned otherwise your sauce will be gritty and burned.

B-There is no need to keep the fish warm while preparing step two because it will be oven poached shortly.

Step two:

A-Do not use the same pan for step two that you used in step one. You will wind up with an extremely bitter sauce because the spices will now burn.

B-Combining the butter and the flour and cooking it is called creating a roux which is a thickening agent. In Cajun cooking, the roux are the darkest roux you will see. These are called brown or golden roux. These are dark, rich gravies.

C-The limas, okra and corn can be either frozen or canned are added at the last minute insures that they are not overcooked.

Note: From step one to step two should take less than twelve minutes.

Pan Smoking

Pan Smoking is the last of the methods we are going to discuss in this book. It's a method I believe that I developed myself. It's a take-off on what I learned in school, something called "quick smoking". In quick smoking and pan smoking, a covered pan is layered with chips of your favorite

Wood chips, put on the top of the stove. The pan is superheated, igniting the wood chips. The pan is then covered with a cover or another pan and the food is placed into the pan, away from he chips. The flame is extinguished then the hot chips and food in the pan are left to smolder, the food will acquire a smoky flavor from the chips.

The seafood can be fully cooked by this method and served on greens as a salad or appetizer or removed partially cooked and oven poached in your favorite sauce. Quick smoking can be used for large pieces of fish such as whole fillets of salmon and is done in a very large pan. Pan smoking is quick smoking adapted to small à la carte portions of seafood.

This method is not really adapted to indoor cooking unless there is a very good ventilation and exhaust system in the kitchen. This is probably the most complex and advanced method discussed in this book. It will make you look like the accomplished chef you should be after having gone through all the steps in this book. Your friends will be amazed at the results you can conjure up. The flavors that pan smoking produces are flavors only produced by a professional working chef like me. But remember, if I can cook, you can cook and tell tall 'Tales' about it, just like me!

Fillets of Yellow fin Tuna over Tricolor Salad with a Soy Vinaigrette

Yield: 2 servings
INGREDIENTS

Preparation step:	Garlic powder	¼ tsp
(Vinaigrette dressing)	Onion powder	¼ tsp
	Ginger powder	¼ tsp
	Sesame seed oil	2Tb
	Soy sauce	¼ cp
	Red wine vinegar	2Tb
	Black pepper	(pinch)
	Sugar	½ tsp

Step one:	Thin sliced yellow fin tuna	4 pc (3 oz ea)
	Olive oil	¼ cp
	Salt and pepper	(to taste)
	Mesquite chips	(a handful)

Step two:	Radicchio	½ cp
(Salad greens)	Arugula	½ cp
	Escarole	½ cp

Nutrition Facts

Amount per Serving
Calories 623.6
Total Fat 42.7 g
Saturated Fat 6.1 g
Polyunsaturated Fat 8.6 g
Monounsaturated Fat 25.6 g
Cholesterol 98.6 mg
Sodium 1,879.2 mg
Potassium 1,046.5 mg
Total Carbohydrate 5.0 g
Dietary Fiber 1.3 g
Sugars 2.1 g
Protein 53.5 g

METHOD

Preparation step: Combine all ingredients to make salad dressing and reserve.

Step one: Dredge the tuna through the oil. Season with the salt and pepper and set aside. Over high heat, heat a sauté pan large enough to accommodate the chips and fish. Place the wood chips in the pan, cover and let the chips ignite and begin to smoke. Remove pan from the fire once the chips are ignited. Place the fish into the pan and cover. Let stand for 2-3 minutes.

Step two: Wash, pat dry and combine the three lettuces. Place upon a platter. Place the tuna on the lettuces and dress with vinaigrette. Serve for lunch.

NOTES

Preparation step:

A-We are making Phil's ever popular soy vinaigrette. You can use any kind dressing you want. I recommend vinaigrette rather than an emulsion. Try this one. You'll like it.

Step one:

A-Heat the pan for approximately one minute then places the chips in it. Do not soak the chips as you might for a regular barbecue.

B-When the chips ignite, push them to the side of the pan so they don't have direct contact with the incoming seafood so you don't get grit and ashes in your food.

C-Covering the product insures the infusion of the smoke flavor into the seafood and will, at this time complete the cooking process.

D-Properly prepared, fresh tuna should be cooked rare or medium and not overcooked. For those who insist on well done tuna, the longer it stays in the pan assures more doneness.

Step two:

A-Any type of greens can be used. The one's in this recipe are endives and are therefore somewhat bitter, so the vinaigrette is an ideal dressing.

Note: From step one to step two should take less than twelve minutes.

Pan Smoked Salmon with Fennel

Yield: 2 servings

INGREDIENTS

Step one:	Salmon fillets	2 pc (6-8 oz)
	Vegetable oil	2tsp
	Salt and pepper	(to taste)
	Hickory Chips	(a handful)
Step two:	Thin sliced fennel	2 cp
	Anisette liquor	1 oz (a shot)
	Melted butter	1 oz
	Chicken stock	1 cp
	Sugar	1tsp
	Salt and pepper	(to taste)

Nutrition Facts

Amount per Serving
Calories 519.5
Total Fat 30.9 g
Saturated Fat 14.2 g
Polyunsaturated Fat 5.1 g
Monounsaturated Fat 7.6 g
Cholesterol 128.7 mg
Sodium 292.4 mg
Potassium 1,321.9 mg
Total Carbohydrate 12.7 g
Dietary Fiber 2.7 g
Sugars 4.0 g
Protein 38.0 g

METHOD

Step one: Dredge the salmon through the oil. Season with the salt and pepper and set aside. Over high heat, heat a sauté pan large enough to accommodate the hickory chips and fish. Place the wood chips in the pan, cover and let the chips ignite and begin to smoke. Remove pan from the fire once the chips are ignited. Place the fish into the pan and cover, let stay for 2-3 minutes.

Step two: In a sauté pan large enough to accommodate the fish, place the fennel, sugar, anisette, chicken stock. Transfer the salmon and place onto the fennel etc. and pour the melted butter over the fish. Season to taste and oven poach for 2-3 minutes longer or until fennel is tender and the salmon flakes easily. Serve salmon on top of the fennel.

NOTES

Step one:

A—Heat pan for, approximately one minute, before placing the chips in it. Do not soak the chips as you might for a regular barbecue.

B-When the chips ignite, push them to the side of the pan so they don't have direct contact with the incoming seafood so you don't get grit and ashes in your food.

C-Recovering the product insures the infusion of the smoke flavor into the seafood and will, at this time complete the cooking process.

Step two:

A-What we are doing here is braising the fennel in a stock sweetened with liquor and sugar.

Note: From step one to step two should take less than twelve minutes.

Stocks

This is the final chapter in our magnum opus. We are discussing here that which we have talked about throughout the book, namely stocks as a cooking medium. The importance of stocks cannot be understated not only because they add flavor and ethnic authenticity but also because they really bring life to the dish.

What is a stock? A stock is a flavored liquid that is used as a cooking medium. One prepares a stock by simmering specific bones and vegetables in a stock pot filled with water, straining the liquid and reducing it to half its volume.

There are a number of different stocks and they are each used for different purposes. Classically speaking, there are white stocks, brown stocks and simple stocks.

A white stock is prepared from the bones of a chicken, a calf or fish.

A brown stock is prepared from the same bones but before the bones and vegetables are simmered, they are roasted in an oven until golden brown.

A simple stock is a stock with containing only vegetables and aromatic herbs. The court bouillon is an example of such a stock.

The strength of a stock depends upon the length of cooking time and the type and quantity of product being simmered. For example, one would not overcook a fish fumet because the longer we cook it, the fishier it's going to get. We are looking for a subtle flavor in fish stocks. On the other hand in preparing a veal or beef stock, the bones are much larger and thus need to cook for a far longer period of time in order to draw the flavor of the bones into the liquid. A chicken stock is somewhere in between. Any stocks can be made from any bones. Rabbit, venison, pheasant are all good for cooking stocks. To increase the strength of any stock, reduce it to one half of its original volume after straining. This is known as a "Demi Glace" and is preferred to a stock when one is going to create a sauce.

People ask what the difference is between a stock and a broth. Simply stated, there is more meat added in a broth. By adding meat with the bones, you are more into a soup stock which is a quicker process than the preparation of a true stock. Broth is very flavorful but lacks the distinction of having the flavor that the bones impart to a liquid.

Making your own stocks is neither as difficult nor as mysterious as many think. All stocks have basically the same recipe. The only thing that varies is the ingredients and the cooking time.

Some nomenclature is required here. There is a combination of vegetables in a 2 to 1 to 1 ratio of onions to carrots to celery known as a "mire poix". The ratio is constant for all stocks. The combination of aromatic herbs added to the liquid is known as a "sachet". The sachet is made of bay leaves, black peppercorns, thyme and parsley in a ration to suit an individual taste. Other herbs can be added. If you make a turkey broth it might behoove you to add some sage. The sachet and mire poix are standard flavoring agents for the simmering bones.

The amount of bones is usually a quart of water per pound of bones. I usually throw as many bones as I can get in a pot and just cover them with water.

Stocks can be preserved by refrigeration for up to one week or can be frozen for extended periods of time. You can use ice cube trays. Usually after two months, they loose quality.

Homemade Vegetable Stock
Court Bouillon

INCORPORATE:

Water	½ gl
Chopped carrot	½ cp
Chopped celery	½ cp
Chopped onions	1cp
Bay leaves	2ea
Black peppercorns	½ tsp
Thyme	½ tsp
Parsley	½ tsp
White wine	1cp

Nutrition Facts

Serving Size: 1cp
Amount per Serving
Calories 29.7
Total Fat 0.2 g
Saturated Fat 0.0 g
Polyunsaturated Fat 0.0 g
Monounsaturated Fat 0.0 g
Cholesterol 0.0 mg
Sodium 55.6 mg
Potassium 149.9 mg
Total Carbohydrate 6.9 g
Dietary Fiber 2.0 g
Sugars 2.5 g
Protein 0.8 g

METHOD
Combine all the ingredients, bring the mixture to a boil, reduce heat and simmer for twenty minutes or until the vegetables are tender and the herbs have released their essences into the broth. Strain, reduce and reserve as a cooking medium.

White Fish Stock (Fumet)

INCORPORATE:

Flounder or sole bones	2 lb
Water	½ gl
Chopped carrot	½ cp
Chopped celery	½ cp
Chopped onions	1cp
Bay leaves	2ea
Black peppercorns	½ tsp
Thyme	½ tsp
Parsley	½ tsp
White wine	1cp

Nutrition Facts

Serving Size: 1 cp
Amount per Serving
Calories 40.0
Total Fat 1.9 g
Saturated Fat 0.5 g
Polyunsaturated Fat 0.3 g
Monounsaturated Fat 0.5 g
Cholesterol 2.0 mg
Sodium 363.0 mg
Potassium 0.0 mg
Total Carbohydrate 0.0 g
Dietary Fiber 0.0 g
Sugars 0.0 g
Protein 5.4 g

METHOD

Step one: Wash the bones well, combine all the ingredients, bring the mixture to a boil, and immediately turn off the heat, let steep for ten minutes. Do not reduce strain and reserve as a cooking medium.

White Chicken Stock

INCORPORATE:

Chicken bones	2 lb
Water	½ gl
Chopped carrot	½ cp
Chopped celery	½ cp
Chopped onions	1cp
Bay leaves	2ea
Black peppercorns	½ tsp
Thyme	½ tsp
Parsley	½ tsp
White wine	1cp

Nutrition Facts

Serving Size: 1 cp
Amount per Serving
Calories 86.4
Total Fat 2.9 g
Saturated Fat 0.8 g
Polyunsaturated Fat 0.5 g
Monounsaturated Fat 1.4 g
Cholesterol 7.2 mg
Sodium 343.2 mg
Potassium 252.0 mg
Total Carbohydrate 8.5 g
Dietary Fiber 0.0 g
Sugars 3.8 g
Protein 6.0 g

METHOD

Step one: Wash the bones well, combine all the ingredients, bring the mixture to a boil, reduce heat and simmer for forty five minutes. Strain and reduce by half, reserve as a cooking medium. If you would prefer a broth (bullion) to a stock, just throw in an old chicken.

White Veal Stock

INCORPORATE:

Veal leg bones	2 lb
Water	½ gl
Chopped carrot	½ cp
Chopped celery	½ cp
Chopped onions	1cp
Bay leaves	2ea
Black peppercorns	½ tsp
Thyme	½ tsp
Parsley	½ tsp
White wine	1cp

Nutrition Facts

Serving size: 1cp
Amount per Serving
Calories 31.2
Total Fat 0.2 g
Saturated Fat 0.1 g
Polyunsaturated Fat 0.0 g
Monounsaturated Fat 0.1 g
Cholesterol 0.0 mg
Sodium 475.2 mg
Potassium 444.0 mg
Total Carbohydrate 2.9 g
Dietary Fiber 0.0 g
Sugars 1.3 g
Protein 4.7 g

METHOD

Step one: Wash the bones and combine all the ingredients, bring the mixture to a boil, reduce heat and simmer for a minimum of two to four hours. Strain, reduce by half and reserve as a cooking medium.

Roasted Brown Stock

INCORPORATE:

Beef or veal bones	2 lb
Tomato paste	2 oz
Chopped carrot	½ cp
Chopped celery	½ cp
Chopped onions	1cp
Water	1gl
Bay leaves	2ea
Black peppercorns	½ tsp
Thyme	½ tsp
Parsley	½ tsp
Red wine	1cp

Nutrition Facts

Serving size: 1 cp
Amount per Serving
Calories 31.2
Total Fat 0.2 g
Saturated Fat 0.1 g
Polyunsaturated Fat 0.0 g
Monounsaturated Fat 0.1 g
Cholesterol 0.0 mg
Sodium 475.2 mg
Potassium 444.0 mg
Total Carbohydrate 2.9 g
Dietary Fiber 0.0 g
Sugars 1.3 g
Protein 4.7 g

METHOD

Step one: Wash the bones well and combine the vegetables, bones and tomato paste in a roasting pan. Roast in a 350 degree oven until golden. Transfer to a stock pot and add the water herbs and wine. Bring the mixture to a boil, reduce heat and simmer for two to four. Strain, reduce by half and reserve as a brown cooking medium.

RECIPE INDEX BY ETHNICITY

Bang-Bang Shrimp—pg 36
Poached Sea Scallops in Port Wine with Cinnamon—pg 43
Poached Fillet of Salmon chilled with a Yogurt Cucumber Dill Sauce—pg 42
Steamed Lobster with Vanilla Butter Sauce—pg 45
Scrod with Mustard and Herbs—pg 51
Trout with Potato Leek Stuffing—pg 54
Barbecued Salmon with Chili Butter—pg 65
Fillets of Yellow fin Tuna over Tricolor Salad with a Soy Vinaigrette—pg 74

GERMAN
Award Winning Monkfish with Sauerkraut and Caraway (NYS Seafood Challenge)—pg 49

MEXICAN
Grilled Shrimp Quesadilla—pg 67

STOCKS
Homemade Vegetable Stock Court Bouillon—pg 78
White Fish Stock (Fumet)—pg 79
White Chicken Stock—pg 80
White Veal Stock—pg 81
Roasted Brown Stock—pg 82

SEAFOOD INDEX

(1) Recipe: **SWORDFISH**—This large food and sport fish average between 200 and 600 pounds. Their mild-flavored, moderately fat flesh is firm, dense and meat-like.

(1) Recipe: **FLOUNDER**—Prized for its fine texture and delicate flavor, it is available whole or in fillets. In America it is often mislabeled as filet of sole.

(1) Recipe: **SOLE**—As a number of flounder family members such as lemon sole, are incorrectly called sole in the United States; true sole is found only in European waters. The best known is the highly prized channel or Dover sole.

(1) Recipe: **LOBSTER**—The most popular variety in the United States is the Maine lobster; also know as the American lobster, they are found off the north-eastern Atlantic coast. Lobsters come in various sizes, the most utilized weight is 1 ¼ to 1 ½ lbs.

(2) Recipe: **SCROD**—Is a young Codfish with mild flavor meat that is white, lean and firm. It's available year round and comes whole or in fillets.

(4) Recipe: **MONKFISH**—Is an extremely ugly angler species that is has low-fat and firm textured flesh. The only edible portion of this fish is the tail and its sweet flavor has been compared to lobster.

(6) Recipe: **SCALLOPS**—Are a bivalve mollusk and even though the entire scallop is edible the portion commonly found in markets is the adductor muscle that hinges the two shells. The larger scallop is known as a Sea or Diver scallops. The smaller, sweeter and more prized are the Bay scallops which are generally found only on the East Coast.

(7) Recipe: **SHRIMP**—This delicious crustacean is America's favorite shellfish. There are hundreds of species that are divided into two categories, warm-water and cold-water, the later being more succulent and smaller. They come in all many of colors including, white, pink and brown.

(3) Recipe: **CATFISH**—Gets its name from its long, whisker-like barbells (feelers). Most are freshwater fish and the majority today is farmed. The flesh is firm, low in fat and mild in flavor.

(2) Recipe: **TUNA**—Is a member of the Mackerel family and is probably the most popular fish used for canning today. There are numerous varieties, Albacore, Blue fin, Yellow fin and Bonito that all are rich flavored, its flesh is moderate to high in fat, firmly textured, flaky and tender.

(4) Recipe: **SALMON**—The population of the once abundant wild Salmon has decreased over the years. Today acquacultured Atlantic salmon is being imported to the United States mostly from Norway, where it has a high-fat flesh content that's pink and succulent.

(1) Recipe **SQUID**—A member of the Cephalopod in the mollusk family it is related to the octopus. The meat has a firm, chewy texture and mild, somewhat sweet flavor. It is also called calamari.

(2) Recipe: **MUSSELS**—Archaeological findings indicate this mollusk has been used as food for over 20,000 years. There are dozens of species, the meat is tougher than that of the clam or oyster but has a delicious, slightly sweet flavor

(4) Recipe: **CLAMS**—The two main varieties of clams are hard-shell and soft-shell. The hard-shell found on the east coast come in three sizes, the smallest are Littlenecks, Cherrystone and Chowder. The most common soft-shell is known as the Steamer.

(1) Recipe: **OYSTERS**-This Bivalve has been a culinary favorite for thousands of years. The hard, rough, gray shell contains a meat that can vary in color from creamy beige to pale grey.

(1) Recipe: **SEA BASS**—A term used to describe any of various saltwater fish. The black bass is a true bass as is the striped bass. In general the flesh is lean to moderately fat; it can be found whole, steaks or fillets.

(1) Recipe: **SNAPPER**—The best known and most popular is the Red Snapper, so named because of its reddish-pink skin and red eyes. Available fresh all year with the peak season in the summer months, the smaller sizes are sold whole, while larger purchased in steaks or fillets.

(1) Recipe: **HALIBUT**—Found in northern Pacific and Atlantic waters, this member of the flatfish family is available al year-round but most abundant from March to September. They can weigh up to half ton, however usually marketed between 50 and 100 pounds as fillets or steaks.

(1) Recipe: **BLUEFISH**—Found along the Atlantic and Gulf coasts, it is nicknamed "bulldog of the ocean" because of its tenacity. It ranges from 3 to 10 pounds and has a fatty, fine-textured flesh which is sold either whole or in fillets.

(1) Recipe: **TROUT**—A large group of fishes belonging to the same family as Salmon. In general, their flesh is firm—textured with medium to high fat content. Probably the best known species is the Rainbow.

(1) Recipe: **CRAB**—Any of a large variety of crustaceans that have 10 legs. The crab used in this recipe is the Blue crab, so named because of its blue claws. It is marketed in both its hard and soft shell stages.

APPENDIX

U.S. Measurement Equivalents

Pinch/dash = 1/16 teaspoon (tsp)
1teaspoon = 1/3 tablespoon (Tb)
3 teaspoons = 1 tablespoon (Tb)
1 tablespoon = 3 teaspoons; 1/2 fluid ounce (oz)
Jigger/shot = 3 tablespoons; 1 1/2 fluid ounces (oz)
4 tablespoons = 2 fluid ounces; 1/4 cup (cp)
8 tablespoons = 4 fluid ounces; 1/2 cup (cp)
16 tablespoons = 8 fluid ounces; 1 cup (cp)
1/8 cup = 2 tablespoons; 1 fluid ounce (oz)
1/4 cup = 4tablespoons; 2 fluid ounces (oz)
1/2 cup = 8 tablespoons; 4 fluid ounces (oz)
3/4 cup = 12 tablespoons; 6 fluid ounces (oz)
1 cup = 16 tablespoons; 8 fluid ounces (oz)
2 cups =16 fluid ounces; 1 pint (pt)
4 cups = 32 fluid ounces; 1 quart (qt)
8 cups = 64 fluid ounces; 2 quart (qt)
1 pint = 16 fluid ounces; 2 cup (cp)
2 pint = 32 fluid ounces; 1 quart (qt)
1 quart = 32 fluid ounces; 4 cup; 2 pint (pt)
4 quart = 128 fluid ounces; 16 cup; 8 pint; 1 gallon (gl)
1 gallon = 128 fluid ounces; 4 quart (qt)
8 quart = 1 peck (pc)